Using
Microsoft Word

2023 Edition

Kevin Wilson

Elluminet Press

www.elluminetpress.com

Using Microsoft Word - 2023 Edition

Publisher: Elluminet Press
Director: Kevin Wilson
Lead Editor: Steven Ashmore
Technical Reviewer: Mike Taylor, Robert Ashcroft
Copy Editors: Joanne Taylor, James Marsh
Proof Reader: Mike Taylor
Indexer: James Marsh
Cover Designer: Kevin Wilson

eBook versions and licenses are also available for most titles. Any source code or other supplementary materials referenced by the author in this text is available to readers at

www.elluminetpress.com/resources

For detailed information about how to locate your book's resources, go to

www.elluminetpress.com/resources

Table of Contents

About the Author

With over 20 years' experience in the computer industry, Kevin Wilson has made a career out of technology and showing others how to use it. After earning a master's degree in computer science, software engineering, and multimedia systems, Kevin has held various positions in the IT industry including graphic & web design, digital film & photography, programming & software engineering, developing & managing corporate networks, building computer systems, and IT support.

He serves as senior writer and director at Elluminet Press Ltd, he periodically teaches computer science at college, and works as an IT trainer in England while researching for his PhD. His books have become a valuable resource among the students in England, South Africa, Canada, and in the United States.

Kevin's motto is clear: "If you can't explain something simply, then you haven't understood it well enough." To that end, he wrote the Exploring Tech Computing series, in which he breaks down complex technological subjects into smaller, easy-to-follow steps that students and ordinary computer users can put into practice.

Microsoft Word

Microsoft Word is a word processing application that allows you to create many different types of document, from letters, Resumes/CVs to greetings cards, posters and flyers. You can select from a library of customisable templates or start from scratch and create your own.

Word gives you the ability to do more with your word processing projects, with the introduction of several enhanced features, such as the ability to create and collaborate on documents online using OneDrive.

Before we begin, throughout this book, we will be using the resource files.

You can download these files from

elluminetpress.com/ms-word

Go down to the 'source files' section and click the icons to download the documents to the documents folder on your PC.

Introduction

Word offers various features and tools to create and edit documents such as text formatting, page layout, and graphics. These tools are all grouped into tabs in a menu system along the top of the screen called a ribbon.

Word uses a WYSIWYG (what-you-see-is-what-you-get) interface, meaning everything you create on screen appears the same way when printed or moved to another app.

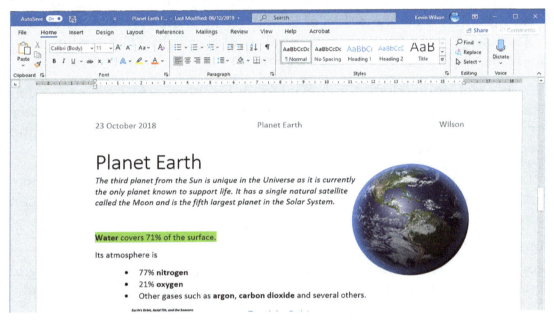

Proofing tools such as spell checkers, grammar check and insight tools allow you to check your work as you type.

Potentially misspelled words are underlined in red, grammar errors are marked in green. Auto-correct features correct commonly misspelled words or phrases.

OneDrive is an online cloud storage service and is integrated with Microsoft Word. This allows you to save your documents directly to OneDrive. This means you can access them from any device, anywhere with an internet connection.

With Microsoft Word's sharing and collaboration features, you and your colleagues can work on the same document simultaneously in real time.

Documents Types

Microsoft Word can be used for many different types of documents such as letters and memos. You can choose fonts, arrange and edit text.

For school and research papers, you can add different styles to keep headings and text the same size and color. A References tab allows you manage your sources and build a bibliography. The spelling and grammar check help catch any mistakes.

When creating marketing material such as flyers and brochures, you can add pictures, shapes, and different text sizes. You can use templates or make your own design. This way, you can make things that grab people's attention.

Building reports, such as those used in business, you can add Headers and Footers, you can keep track of page numbers and titles. You can also add charts and tables to show data in an easy-to-read way.

When putting together manuals and guides, you can add table of contents where readers can find what they need fast. You can also add pictures and keep text consistent to make things easy to understand.

Document Formats

Microsoft Word allows you to save documents in various file formats, each serving a different purpose and suitable for various uses.

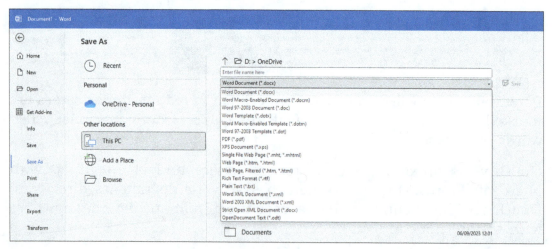

.docx is the standard document format for Word 2007 and later versions, it preserves formatting and enables file sharing when users have different versions of Word. This is the format you should save all your Word documents in.

.dotx is the format you use for saving any Word templates that you create yourself.

.dotm is the format you use for saving standard Word templates that contain macros and other scripting such as automating formatting processes, or performing automated calculations.

.doc is a legacy document version used in older versions of Word. Useful for compatibility.

.pdf is a universal format for sharing documents while preserving formatting, images, and fonts. These files are viewable on various devices without the need for Word but are not easily editable without specific software.

.rtf is a Rich Text Format that allows for basic formatting. These files can be opened by almost any word processor, making it suitable for broad file sharing, but may lack more advanced formatting features.

.txt is a plain text file without any formatting. These files can be opened with any text editor but does not support any formatting or images.

.odt is a text document format for OpenDocument, used by some open-source word processing software such as open office or libre office.

.html is a format for creating web pages. Note the html file itself doesn't not contain images. Any embedded images, audio, or video will be saved in a separate folder.

.mhtml is a web page archive format that stores images and other resources in a single file.

When creating standard documents such as letters, papers, reports, or those for collaborative endeavors the ".docx" format would be used.

If a document is to be distributed for reading purposes only, where the preservation of formatting, fonts, and imagery across various platforms is vital, a ".pdf" format would used.

If you are going to send the document to someone who uses another word processing application such as Libre Office, then the ".rtf" or ".odt" format may be used for example.

2

Getting Started

In this chapter, we'll explore the functionalities and mechanics of the Microsoft Word interface We'll look at:

- Starting Word
- The Main Screen
- The Ribbon
- Home Ribbon Tab
- Insert Ribbon Tab
- Design Ribbon Tab
- Page Layout Ribbon Tab
- References Ribbon Tab
- Review Ribbon Tab
- Mailings Ribbon Tab
- View Ribbon Tab
- Format Ribbon Tab
- File Backstage
- Page Rulers
- Zoom Controls
- Quick Access Toolbar
- Tell Me Feature

To help you better understand this section, take a look at the video resources. Open your web browser and navigate to the following website:

elluminetpress.com/start-word

Starting Word

The quickest way to start Microsoft Word is to search for it using the search field on the bottom left of your task bar. Type "Word". From the search results, click 'word'. You'll also find it on your start menu.

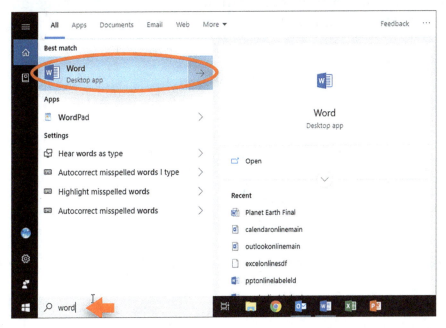

Once Word has started, you'll land on the home screen. On the home screen, you'll see recently used templates along the top, and your most recently saved documents listed underneath.

To begin, click 'blank document' to start. This will open up Word with a new document for you.

The Main Screen

Once you have selected a template or created a new document, you will see your main work screen.

On the bottom left of the main window you'll see your page and word counter, as well as your language selection tools.

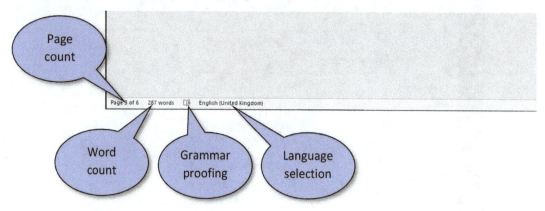

If you click on the page count you'll see your document navigation side bar.

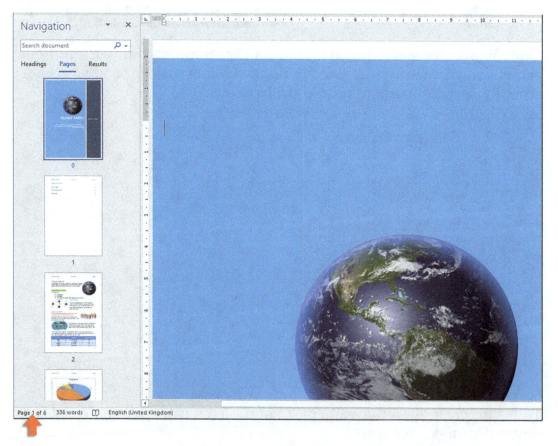

Click on the word count on the bottom left and you'll see some statistics

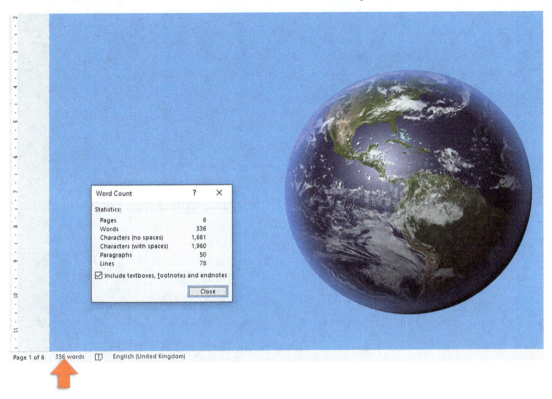

Click on the grammar and proofing icon on the bottom left to open grammar and spell check.

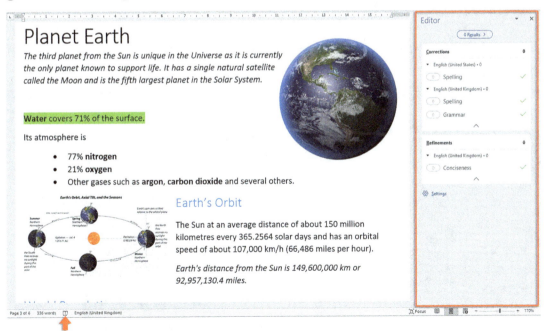

Here you can run through your spelling and grammar.

Click on the language selection icon to change your proofing language.

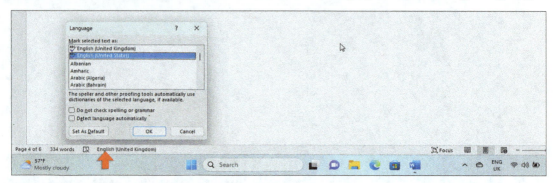

On the bottom right hand side of the screen, you'll see your document display modes: reading, print & web.

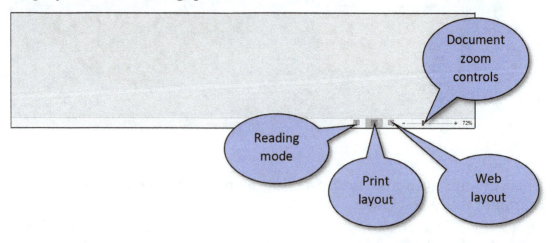

For normal documents it is best to leave the display mode on print layout.

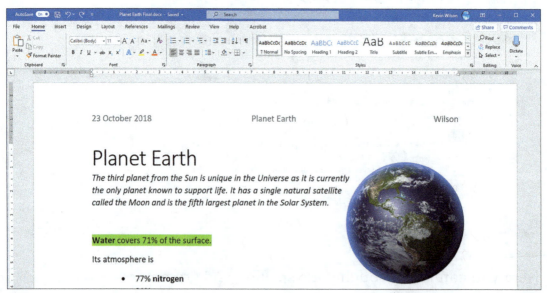

To read through your document you can use reading mode.

You can also use web mode if you intend to publish your document as a webpage on a blog or website.

The Ribbon

Along the top of the screen, all the tools used in Microsoft Word are organised into a ribbon which is divided into ribbon tabs, each containing a specific set of tools.

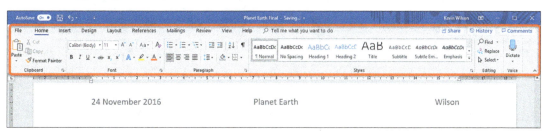

Home Ribbon Tab

You will find your text formatting tools here for making text bold, changing style, font, paragraph alignment etc.

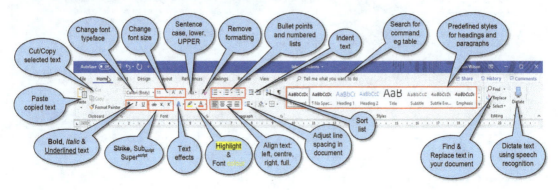

Insert Ribbon Tab

This is where you will find your clip-art, tables, pictures, page breaks, and pretty much anything you would want to insert into a document.

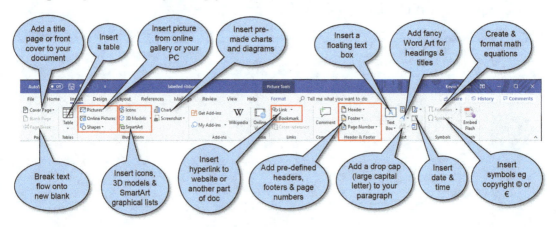

Design Ribbon Tab

Anything to do with pre-set themes and formatting, such as headings, colors and fonts that you can apply to your document and word will automatically format your document according to the themes.

Just select a theme from the options.

Page Layout Ribbon Tab

On this ribbon, you will find your page sizes, margins, page orientation (landscape or portrait) and anything to do with how your page is laid out.

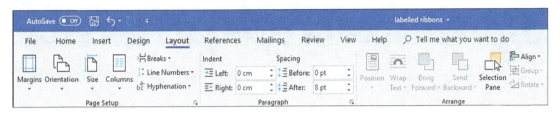

References Ribbon Tab

This is where you can add automatically generated tables of contents, indexes, footnotes to your documents. You can also use reference tools such as researcher and smart lookup to find information about certain topics and phrases used in your documents.

Review Ribbon Tab

On the review ribbon, you'll find document proofing tools such as word count, spelling, thesaurus and dictionary. As well as language settings, and language translation tools.

Mailings Ribbon Tab

From the mailings ribbon you can print mailing labels, print on envelopes and create mail-merge documents from a list of names & addresses.

View Ribbon Tab

On the view ribbon you'll find tools to help you navigate around your document. You can zoom into the document, view as multiple pages side by side, as well as adjusting your page rulers, and the navigation pane.

Format Ribbon Tab

The format ribbon only appears when you have selected an image in your document.

From here you can remove an image background - this only works if the image has a solid black or white background. You can correct the colors using the brightness and contrast 'corrections'.

You can add picture styles such as borders, shadows and outlines.

You can also wrap your text around your image using the text wrap feature. You can also bring a textbox or image to the front if it falls behind a block of text and rotate an image. Similarly with 'send to back', you can send an image behind a block of text or another image.

You can crop an image and set the height and width of the image if you have an exact size.

File Backstage

If you click 'File' on the top left of your screen, this will open up what Microsoft call the backstage.

Backstage is where you open or save documents, print documents, export or share documents, as well as options, Microsoft account and preference settings.

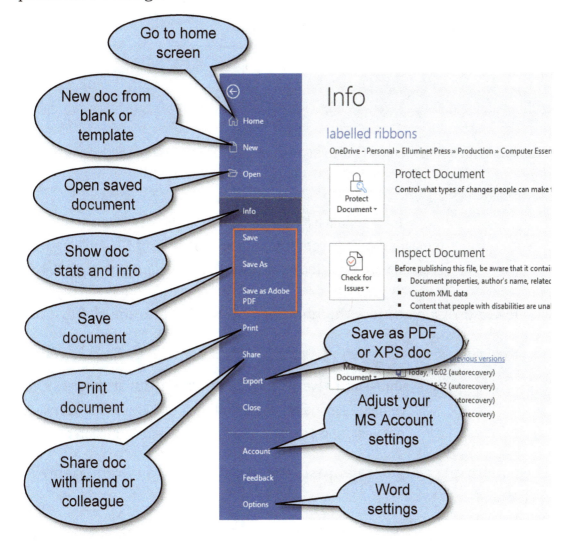

You can also change your Microsoft Account settings, log in and activate your Microsoft Office Suite, change Word's preferences and so on.

Page Rulers

Along the top of your page you'll see your page ruler. This will indicate your page width, show any tabs or margins on your page.

There are three markers on the left hand side worth noting. You can drag these to adjust your margin or text indent.

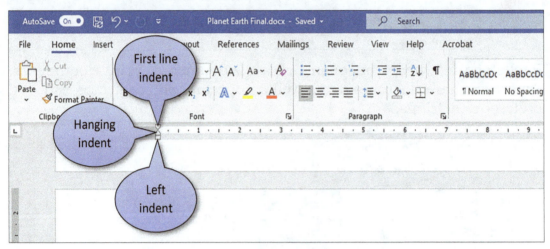

The top triangle adjusts the first line indent. Drag over to the right.

Total annual births were highest in the late 1980s at about 13 remain essentially constant at their 2011 level of 135 million, while year, and are expected to increase to 80 million per year by 2040.

The lower triangle adjusts the hanging indent. Drag to the right.

Total annual births were highest in the late 1980s at about 139 milli remain essentially constant at their 2011 level of 135 million, per year, and are expected to increase to 80 million per year

The square on the bottom adjusts the left indent. Drag to the right.

Total annual births were highest in the late 1980s at about 13 remain essentially constant at their 2011 level of 135 million, per year, and are expected to increase to 80 million per year

Zoom Controls

You can quickly adjust your zoom using the controls on the bottom right of your screen. Shift the slider to the right to zoom in, and to the left to zoom out.

You can also zoom using the controls on the view ribbon. Click 'zoom'.

From the dialog box, select your zoom level: 100%, 200%, etc.

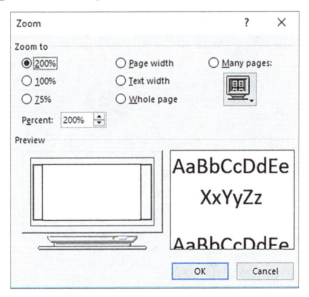

Zoom to 'page width' and 'whole document' are worth keeping in mind.

'Zoom to page width', zooms into your document to the width of the page giving you a clear view of your document and is useful for editing and reading.

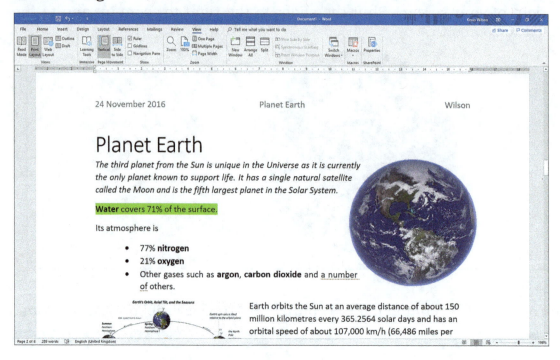

'Zoom to whole document', zooms out to show the whole document on the screen at a time. This helps when you want to see what your document looks like at full page.

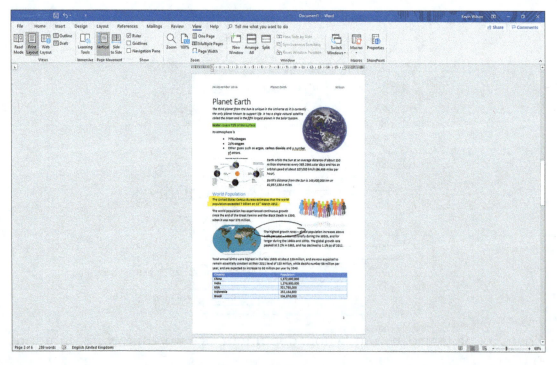

Quick Access Toolbar

The Quick Access Toolbar provides quick and easy access to frequently used commands and functions with just a click. You'll find it on the top left of the title bar in the main window.

By default, the Quick Access Toolbar contains only a few commonly used commands such as Save, Undo, and Redo.

If you want to add a command, right-click on any command in the ribbon then select 'Add to Quick Access Toolbar'. For example, if you wanted to add the 'pictures' command from the 'insert' ribbon.

You'll see the command appear on the toolbar.

If you want to remove a command, right-click on it and choose "Remove from Quick Access Toolbar."

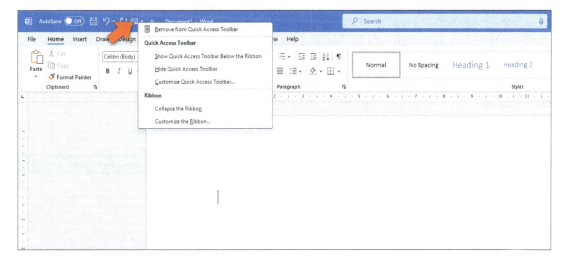

For more convenience, you can also move this toolbar under the ribbon. To do this, right click on the toolbar, then select 'show quick access toolbar below the ribbon'.

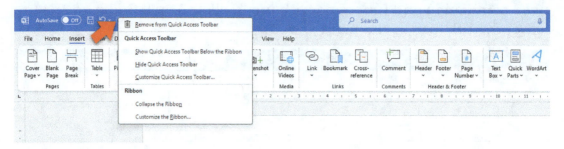

The bar will appear below the ribbon.

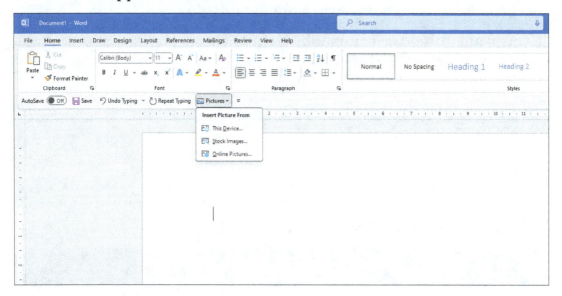

Tell Me Feature

The "Tell Me" feature in Microsoft Word is a powerful search tool that can help you quickly find and access various commands, functions, and features within Microsoft Word. You can locate specific actions or tools, especially when you're not sure where to find them in the Ribbon or menus.

You can find this field on the top of the menu bar.

Type a command in to the field. For example, if I wanted to insert a picture, type 'insert picture' into the search field.

From the drop down menu that appears, click on the command you were looking for.

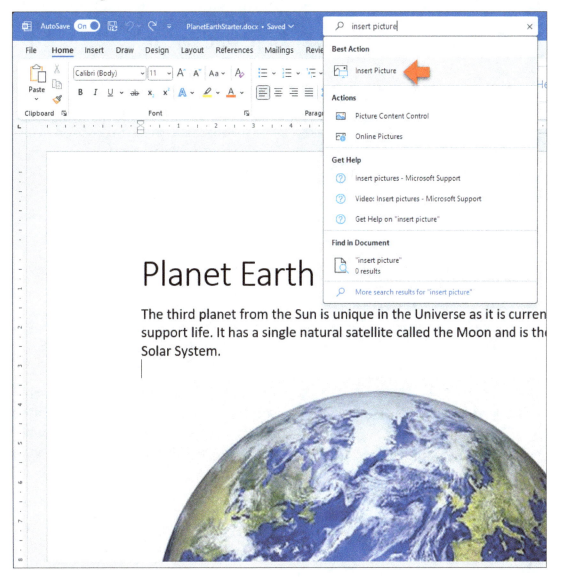

This feature can be used in all the Office Apps. If you can't find the tool on the menus or ribbons, just search for it.

3

Building Documents

In this chapter, we'll explore how to create documents, edit and format text. We'll look at:

- Building Documents
- Creating a New Document
- Bold, Italic & Underlined
- Superscript & Subscript
- Highlighting Text
- Text Color
- Change Case
- Paragraph Styles
- Editing Paragraph Styles
- Custom Styles
- Text Justification
- Paragraph Indents
- Paragraph Spacing
- Line Spacing
- Contents Pages & Indexes
- Search & Replace

To help you better understand this section, take a look at the video resources. Open your web browser and navigate to the following website:

elluminetpress.com/word-docs

You'll also need to download the source files from:

elluminetpress.com/word

Creating a New Document

To create a new blank document, click 'file' on the top left of your screen,

Select 'new', then double click the 'blank document' thumbnail.

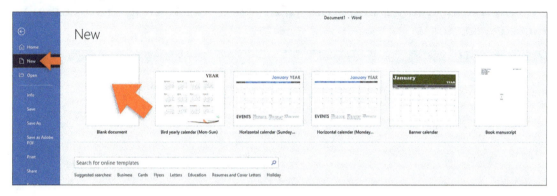

Entering Text

Use your keyboard to type in your text. You'll see a small flashing bar called a cursor (circled below). This tells you were the text will appear when you type.

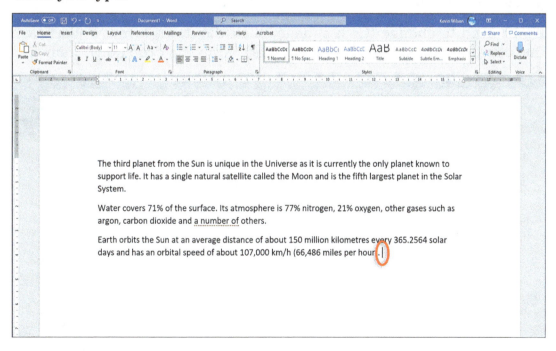

Dictate Text

If you have a microphone on your computer, you can dictate text. To do this, open a blank document. From the home ribbon click 'dictate'.

The icon will change indicating that word is listening. You can now dictate your text.

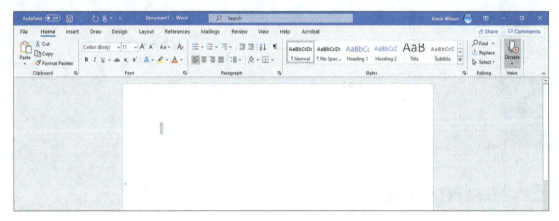

You can add punctuation using keywords such as "period" or "comma". Use "new line" to start on a new line in your document, and "new paragraph" to start a new paragraph of text.

If you need to change the language, click the down arrow underneath the 'dictate' icon and select the language from the drop down menu.

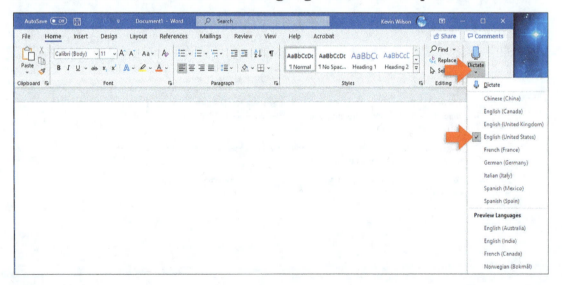

Selecting Text

To select text, click and drag your mouse over the text you want to select. The selected text with be highlighted in grey.

PLANET EARTH

The third planet from the Sun is unique in the Universe as it is currently the only planet known to support life. It has a single natural satellite called the Moon and is the fifth largest planet in the Solar System.

Water covers 71% of the surface. Its atmosphere is 77% nitrogen, 21% oxygen, other gases such as argon, carbon dioxide and a number of c

Earth orbits the Sun at an average distance of about 150 million kilometres every 365.2564 solar days and has an orbital speed of about 107,000 km/h (66,486 miles per hour).

To quickly select a line, click next to the line in the margin of the document.

PLANET EARTH

 The third planet from the Sun is unique in the Universe as it is currently the only planet known to support life. It has a single natural satellite called the Moon and is the fifth largest planet in the Solar System.

Water covers 71% of the surface. Its atmosphere is 77% nitrogen, 21% oxygen, other gases such as argon, carbon dioxide and a number of others.

Earth orbits the Sun at an average distance of about 150 million kilometres every 365.2564 solar days and has an orbital speed of about 107,000 km/h (66,486 miles per hour).

To quickly select a paragraph, double click next to the paragraph in the margin of the document.

PLANET EARTH

 The third planet from the Sun is unique in the Universe as it is currently the only planet known to support life. It has a single natural satellite called the Moon and is the fifth largest planet in the Solar System.

Water covers 71% of the surface. Its atmosphere is 77% nitrogen, 21% oxygen, other gases such as argon, carbon dioxide and a number of others.

Earth orbits the Sun at an average distance of about 150 million kilometres every 365.2564 solar days and has an orbital speed of about 107,000 km/h (66,486 miles per hour).

You can also double click on a word to select it.

Bold, Italic & Underlined

You can use **bold**, *italic* or <u>underlined</u> text to emphasise certain words or paragraphs.

Just select the text you want to apply formatting to and from the home ribbon select one of the icons: **bold**, *italic* or <u>underlined</u>.

For example, I want to make the text "water", "nitrogen" and "oxygen" bold. To do this, double click on the word to highlight it.

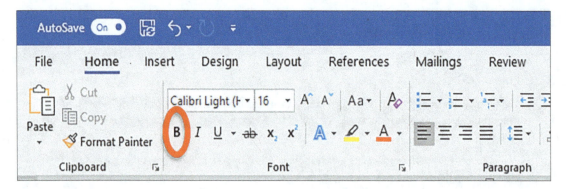

Click the bold icon on your home ribbon. Do this for each of the individual words.

Do the same for <u>underlined</u> and *italic* text, using the appropriate icons on the home ribbon.

Try changing some text to italic or underlined.

Superscript & Subscript

Subscripts appear below the text line and are used primarily in mathematical formulas, to express chemical compounds or footnotes.

For example.

H_2O or CO_2

You can add subscripts to your text. To do this, first highlight the character you want to make into a subscript. In this example, I want to select the '2' in H20.

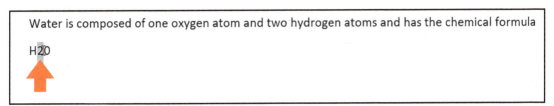

Click your mouse before the '2' and drag over to the right until the '2' is highlighted in grey, as shown above. Click the subscript icon on your home ribbon.

Superscripts appear at the top of the text line and are used primarily in mathematical formulas or to express chemical compounds.

For example:

Temperature was **32°C**, or the area of the circle is = **πr^2**

For superscripts, it's the same procedure except you select superscript from the home ribbon, instead of subscript.

Give it a try.

If the subscript or superscript icons aren't there, click the expand icon at the bottom right of the font section of the home ribbon, circled below at the top of the screen print.

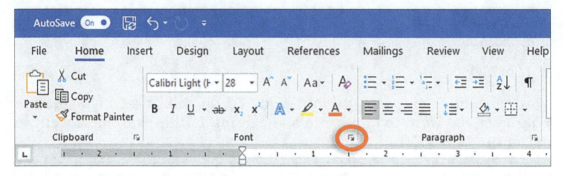

In the dialog box that appears, select subscript or superscipt option under the 'effects' section, then click ok.

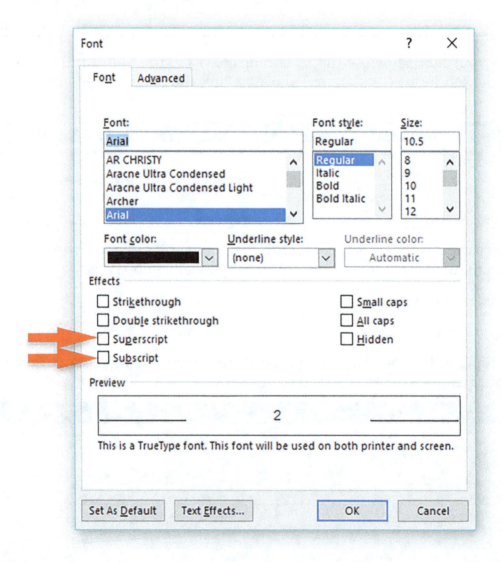

Highlighting Text

To highlight text, first click the small down arrow next to the highlight icon on your home ribbon.

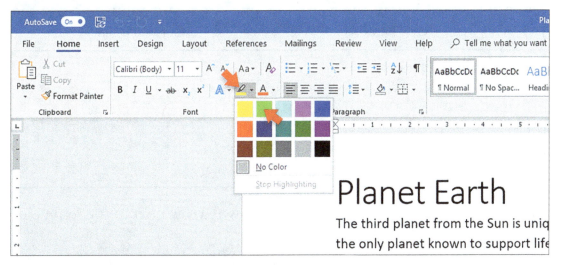

From the drop down menu that appears, select a color. Usually yellow, green or turquoise show up well.

Now with the highlight tool, click and drag it across the text you want to highlight. In this example, I want to highlight 'Water covers 71% of the surface.'

Planet Earth

The third planet from the Sun is unique in the Universe as it is currently the only planet known to support life. It has a single natural satellite called the Moon and is the fifth largest planet in the Solar System.

Water covers 71% of the surface.

Its atmosphere is

Once you release your mouse, you'll see the text highlight in the color you chose.

called the Moon and is the fifth largest planet in the Solar System.

Water covers 71% of the surface.

To turn off the highlight tool, click the icon again on your home ribbon.

Text Color

To change the color of the text, first highlight it with your mouse. In the example below, I want to change the text color of the first paragraph. To do this, click before the word 'the' and drag your mouse across the paragraph, to the end after 'March 2012', to highlight it.

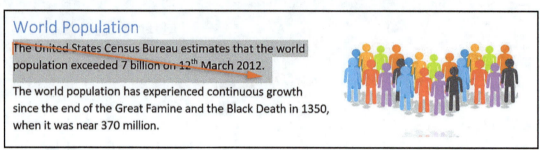

From the home ribbon, click the small down arrow next to the font color icon.

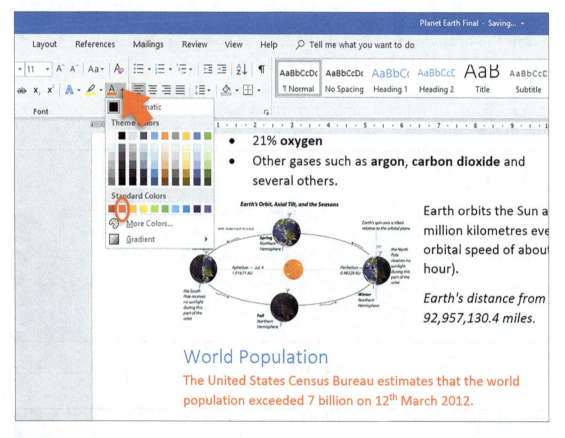

From the drop down menu that appears, select the color you want from the palette.

Once you click on a color, the selected text will change.

Change Case

You can change the case of a word or sentence using the change case feature. You can use:

Sentence case

lowercase text

UPPERCASE TEXT

Capitalise Each Word

To change the case of a word or sentence, first highlight it with your mouse.

Planet earth

The third planet from the Sun is unique in the Universe as it is currently the only planet known to support life. It has a single natural satellite called the Moon and is the fifth largest planet in the Solar System.

Water covers 71% of the surface. Its atmosphere is 77% nitrogen, 21% oxygen, other gases such as argon, carbon dioxide and a number of others.

Earth orbits the Sun at an average distance of about 150 million kilometres every 365.2564 solar days and has an orbital speed of about 107,000 km/h (66,486 miles per hour).

From the home ribbon tab, select the case icon. From the drop down menu, select the case you want to change to. Eg uppercase.

The selected text will change accordingly.

PLANET EARTH

The third planet from the Sun is unique in the Universe as it is currently the only planet known to support life. It has a single natural satellite called the Moon and is the fifth largest planet in the Solar System.

Water covers 71% of the surface. Its atmosphere is 77% nitrogen, 21% oxygen, other gases such as argon, carbon dioxide and a number of others.

Earth orbits the Sun at an average distance of about 150 million kilometres every 365.2564 solar days and has an orbital speed of about 107,000 km/h (66,486 miles per hour).

Paragraph Styles

Word has a number of paragraph styles that are useful for keeping your formatting consistent. The idea is to format all your headings with 'title', 'heading 1', 'heading 2', 'heading 3', your main text as 'normal', and so on. This makes it easier to format your document so you don't have to apply the same font style, size and color manually every time you want a heading.

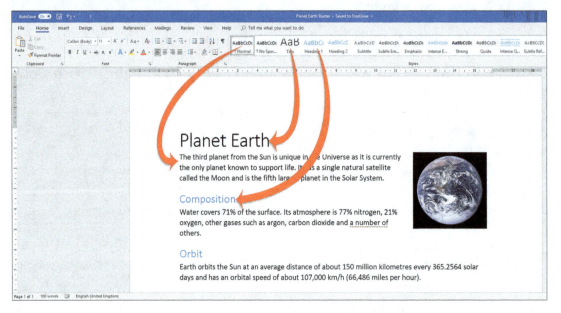

To apply the styles to a heading or paragraph, highlight it with your mouse as shown below.

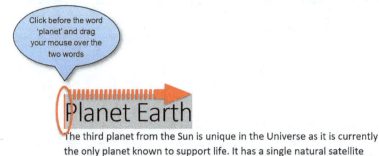

Select the style from the home ribbon.

Editing Paragraph Styles

To edit a style, right click on the style you want to edit. As an example, I'm going to change the font size of 'heading 1'. First, right click the 'heading 1' style on your home ribbon, then from the drop down menu, click 'modify'.

From the dialog box, under the 'formatting' section, you'll see font typeface and font size. Make your changes here. I'm going with size 16 instead of 18.

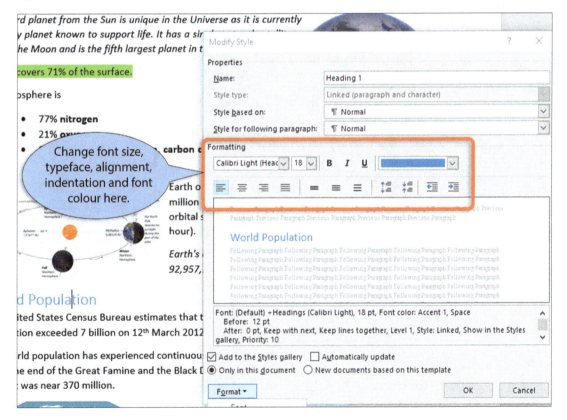

To change anything else, go down to the 'format' button at the bottom left of the dialog box.

From the drop down menu, you can change your paragraph spacing, line spacing, borders and text effects. Select the appropriate option from the menu.

In the example, I am changing the paragraph spacing, ie the spacing before and after the heading.

To change this setting, select 'paragraph' from the drop down format menu, and adjust the settings in the 'spacing' section of the dialog box that appears.

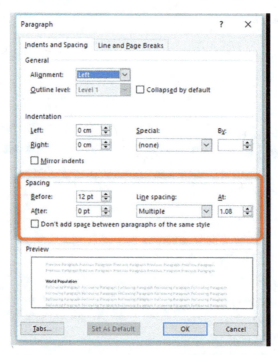

I want 12pts before each heading, so enter 12pt in the 'before' field. This will space out the sections in my document, leaving a gap before each heading.

Try some of the other settings. Try adding a text effect or a border.

Custom Styles

Creating custom styles in Microsoft Word allows you to develop a personalized and consistent formatting template that you can apply throughout your document. This can be particularly useful for maintaining a professional and uniform appearance in your texts.

To do this, go to the 'home' tab, open the 'styles' side panel. Click on small icon on the bottom right of the styles section.

A side panel on the right hand side will open. Click the 'new style' icon at the bottom.

A formatting dialog box will appear. Give the style a meaningful name.

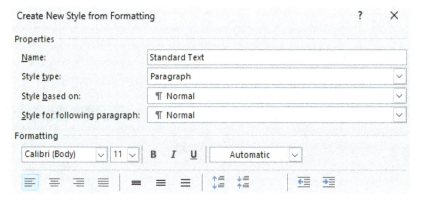

Define the style type (paragraph, character, table, or list) in the "Style type" dropdown menu.

If your new style is similar to an existing one, you can choose it in the "Style based on" dropdown to save time.

If you want your text to automatically shift to another style after a paragraph in your new style is completed, select an option in the "Style for following paragraph" dropdown.

Now define your custom style. Click on the 'Format' button in the bottom-left corner of the dialog box.

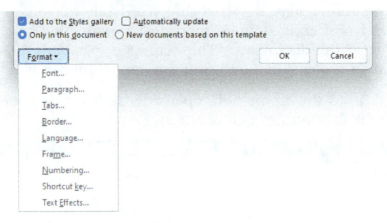

From the drop down menu, choose the aspect of the style you want to customize - font, paragraph, tabs, border, etc.

- **Font:** Define the typeface, size, color, and other font attributes.

- **Paragraph:** Set alignment, indentation, spacing, and other paragraph attributes.

- **Tabs:** Set tab stops and their alignment.

- **Border:** Choose border style, color, width, and where it appears.

- **Numbering:** Define the format for ordered or unordered lists.

Once you're done, click 'ok'.

You'll be able to apply the style using the styles section in the home tab.

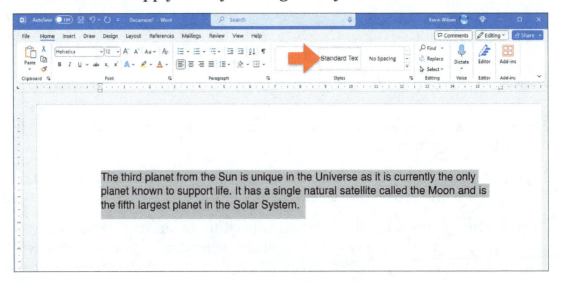

Text Justification

Text justification is the alignment of text relative to the margins on a page. You can align text to the left or right margins, or centred between margins, as shown below.

Most text will be **left aligned** as demonstrated in this paragraph. Only the left margin is aligned, the right margin is not.

Text can also be **right aligned**
this is good for addresses on the top of letters

Text can also be **fully justified**. This means that the left and right margins are both aligned. This helps when creating documents with images, as the text will line up neatly around the image.

Text can also be **centre aligned**,
as demonstrated by this paragraph and
is good for headings, verses,
poems and so on.

To justify paragraphs, first select the text you want to apply the formatting to.

In this example, I want fully justify the first paragraph. This means the text is aligned on both the left and right margins.

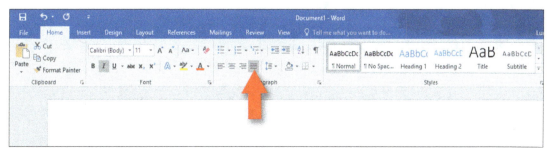

Select the text, then from the home ribbon select the fully justify icon.

Paragraph Indents

To increase the indent of a paragraph, select the text with your mouse so it's highlighted.

Earth's atmosphere is made up of

77% **nitrogen,** 21% **oxygen** and other gases such as **argon, carbon dioxide** and several others which make up the other 2%.

Earth orbits the Sun at an average distance of about 150 million kilometres every 365.2564 solar days and has an orbital speed of about 107,000 km/h (66,486 miles per hour).

From your home ribbon, click the increase indent icon.

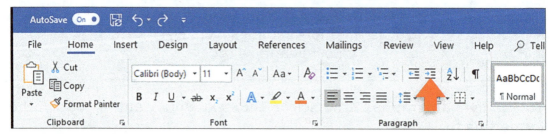

This will produce something like this. This makes it easier to read the information in the document.

Earth's atmosphere is made up of

77% **nitrogen,** 21% **oxygen** and other gases such as **argon, carbon dioxide** and several others which make up the other 2%.

Earth orbits the Sun at an average distance of about 150 million kilometres every 365.2564 solar days and has an orbital speed of about 107,000 km/h (66,486 miles per hour).

To decrease the indent, just use the decrease indent icon instead.

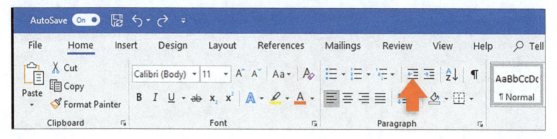

First Line Indent

The first line indent is a good way to begin paragraphs. This helps the reader to process the information and to identify sections in your text.

A first line indent, indents the first line of a paragraph with all other lines of text in line with the left margin.

First, select the paragraph you want to indent. Then click the expand icon under the paragraph section of the home ribbon.

In the paragraph dialog box, go down to 'indentation', and in the 'special' drop down field, select 'first line'.

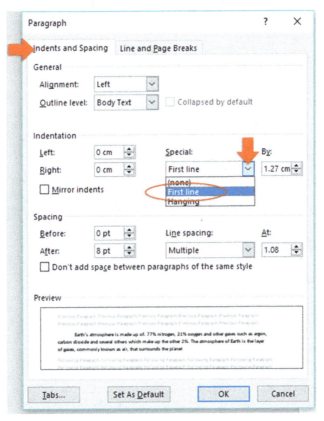

Click OK.

Hanging Indent

A hanging indent, indents all the lines except the first one. These indents are usually used with lists, bullet points or bibliographies.

Wilson. K (2016, March 4). Using Microsoft Office 2016: *Getting Started With* Word, *p34, Chapter 4.* Retrieved from   http://www.elluminetpress.com

First, select the paragraph you want to indent. Then click the expand icon under the paragraph section of the home ribbon.

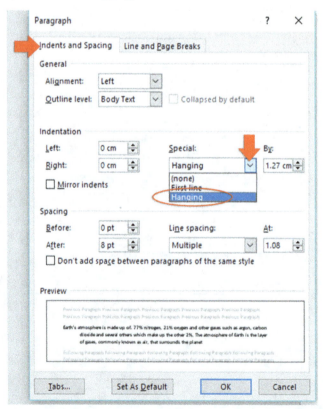

In the paragraph dialog box, go down to 'indentation' and in the 'special' drop down field, select 'hanging'.

Click OK.

Paragraph Spacing

Paragraph spacing is the space before and after a paragraph. Space and font size is measured in points (pt).

First, select the paragraph you want to adjust. Then click the expand icon under the paragraph section of the home ribbon.

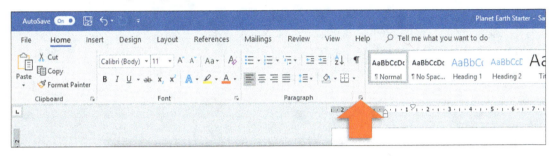

Under the 'spacing' section of the 'indents and spacing' tab, you'll see 'before' and 'after'.

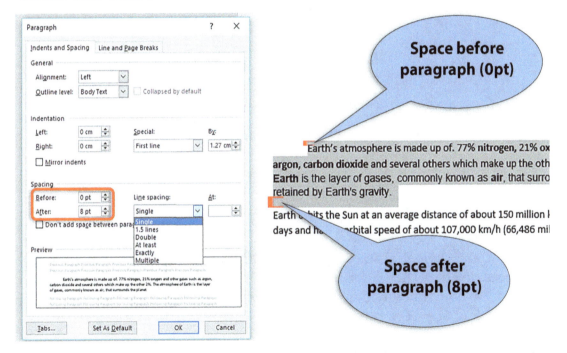

This is where you can adjust the spacing. In this example, I have entered 8pts after the selected paragraph.

This means that there will be an 8pt gap after the paragraph on the page, as you can see above.

These settings are usually applied to the paragraph styles, but you can adjust them here.

Line Spacing

Line spacing is the space between each line. Space and font size is measured in points (pt).

First, select the paragraph you want to adjust. Then click the expand icon under the paragraph section of the home ribbon.

Under spacing on the 'indents and spacing' tab, go down to 'line spacing'.

Here you can select single, this is the default. Double, this as its name suggests doubles the space between the lines. 1.5 lines makes the space one and a half times wider. If you select 'at least', you can specify the size of the space between the lines.

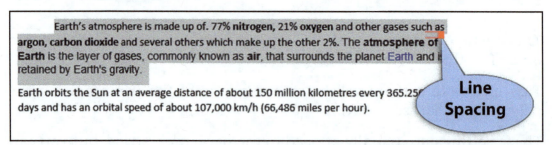

These settings are usually applied to the paragraph styles.

Tabs

To access tab settings, go to your home ribbon and click the expand icon on the bottom right of the paragraph section. From the dialog box that appears, click 'tabs' on the bottom left.

Now from this box, you can add tab stops. If you look along the ruler at the top of the document, you'll see some measurements.

For this particular document, I'm entering finish times and I want all the times to line up in the list (about 5cm across the page should be enough for the first column).

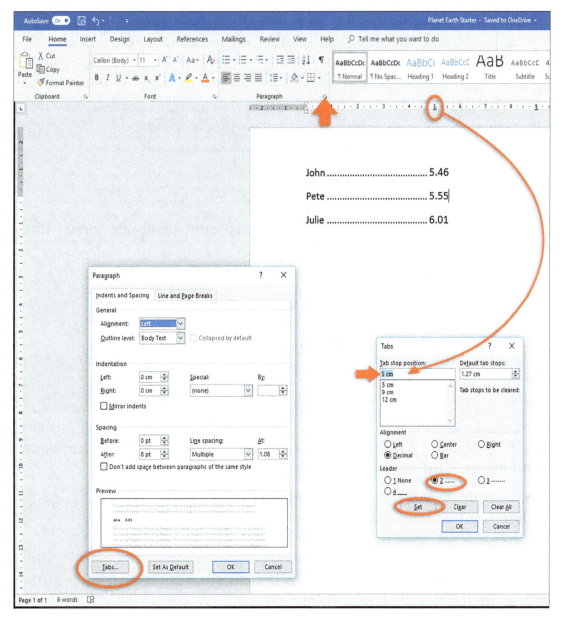

In the 'tab stop position' field enter 5cm. Set the alignment of the tab. Note there are different types of tabs.

Left aligned tabs align all text to the left against the tap stop. **Decimal tabs** align all the decimal points in the numbers, in-line with the tab stop and are good for displaying numbers. **Centre aligned tabs** align all the text centre to the tab stop. **Right aligned tabs** align all text to the right against the tab stop. See the image below.

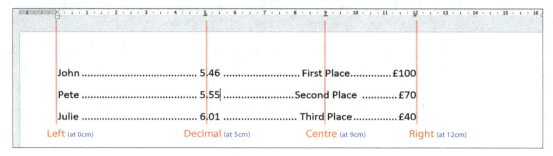

Decimal tabs would work well for the column of finish times. Click 'decimal' under the alignment section.

I also want some leading dots to make it easier to read. So in the 'leader' section, click the second option.

Now repeat the process and add the tabs at 9cm and 12cm, noting the different tab alignments (left, decimal, centre, right).

Click OK when done.

Now, every time you press the tab key on your keyboard, your cursor will jump to the tab stop position.

Bullet Lists

Edit the document and change the sentence explaining atmospheric composition to a bullet point list. Select the text using your mouse as shown below.

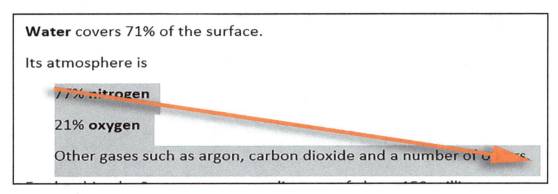

Then from your home ribbon, click the bullet points icon.

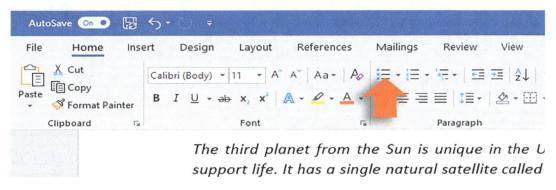

You can also have different styles of bullets: ticks, stars, shapes, and so on. To get the drop down menu, click the small down arrow next to the bullet icon.

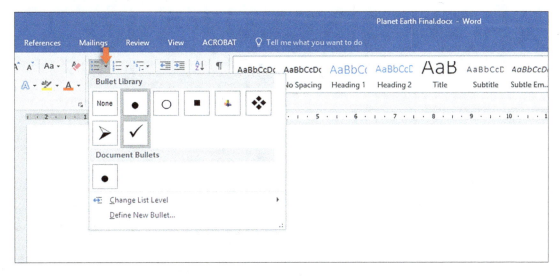

Numbered Lists

Edit the document and change the sentence explaining atmospheric composition to a numbered point list. Select the text using your mouse as shown below.

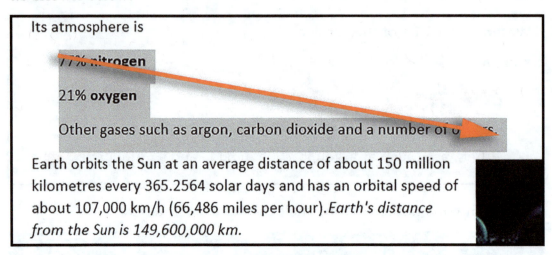

From the home ribbon, click the numbered list icon.

You can also have different styles of numbered lists. To get the drop down menu, click the small down arrow next to the numbered list icon.

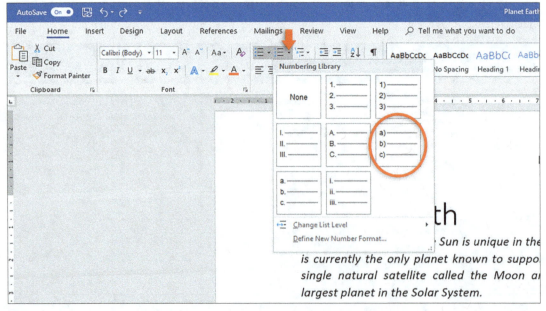

Sorting Text

You can easily sort a list of items into ascending or descending order. For example, I want to alphabetise the list of names below.

First highlight the names as shown above, then click the sort icon on the home ribbon

Now, if we use the default sort settings, the list will be sorted by the first letter of each line of text.

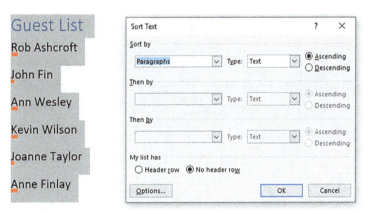

In most cases this is ok, but in this case I want to sort the names by surname. Remember, word sees the list as the first name as word 1 and the surname as word 2.

To change the sort options, click options at the bottom of the dialog box.

Select 'other' and in the small text field enter a space using the spacebar on your keyboard. Then click 'ok'.

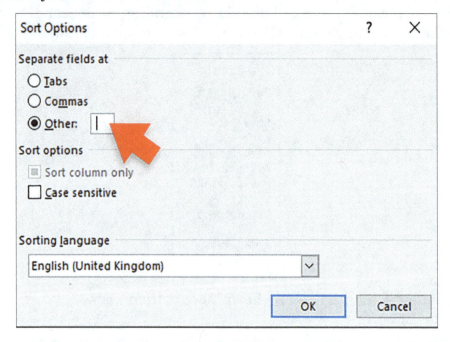

Now, in the 'sort text' dialog box, go down to the 'sort by' section, and in the first field, select 'word 2' - remember word 2 is the surname, this is what we want to sort the list by.

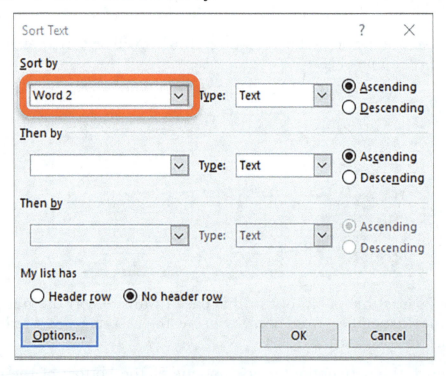

Click 'ok' when you're done.

Cross-Referencing

Cross-referencing in Word allows you to link to other parts of the same document, which can be particularly useful for creating a cohesive and interconnected document. This feature is often used in larger documents to help navigate to related sections, figures, tables, or footnotes without having to scroll through pages.

Place your cursor where you want the cross-reference to appear in your document.

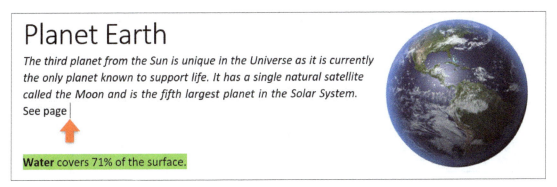

Go to the 'References' tab, click on "Cross-reference".

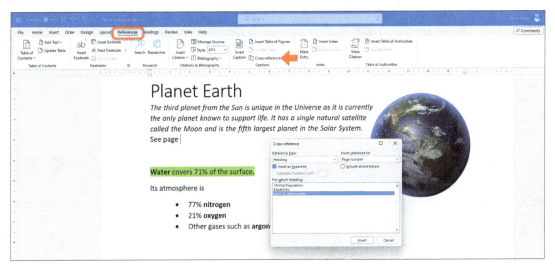

In the "Cross-reference" dialog box, select the type of item you are referencing from the "Reference type" dropdown menu. In this example I want to reference a heading on another page.

Choose the type of reference information to display in the "Insert reference to" dropdown menu. In this case I want to show the page number the section is on.

You can do the same with tables, figures and paragraphs.

Cut, Copy & Paste

To ease editing documents, you can use copy, cut and paste to move paragraphs or pictures around in different parts of your document.

First select the paragraph below with your mouse by clicking before the word 'Earth', and dragging your mouse across the line towards the end of the line, as shown below.

The third planet from the Sun is unique in the Universe as it is currently the only planet known to support life. It has a single natural satellite called the Moon and is the fifth largest planet in the Solar System. Earth's distance from the sun is 149,600,000 km.

Click & drag across text to highlight

Once you have done that, click 'cut' from the left hand side of your home ribbon. This will 'cut out' the paragraph.

Now click on the position in the document you want the paragraph you just cut out to be inserted.

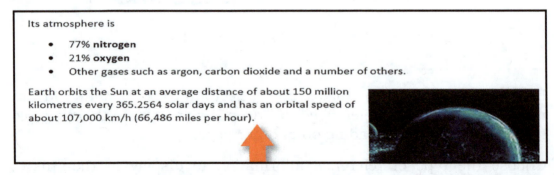

Its atmosphere is

- 77% **nitrogen**
- 21% **oxygen**
- Other gases such as argon, carbon dioxide and a number of others.

Earth orbits the Sun at an average distance of about 150 million kilometres every 365.2564 solar days and has an orbital speed of about 107,000 km/h (66,486 miles per hour).

Once you have done that click 'paste' from the home ribbon. If you wanted to copy something ie make a duplicate of the text, then use the same procedure except click 'copy' instead of 'cut'.

Using the Clipboard

You'll find Word's clipboard on the home ribbon. Just click the small icon under the clipboard section on the left hand side.

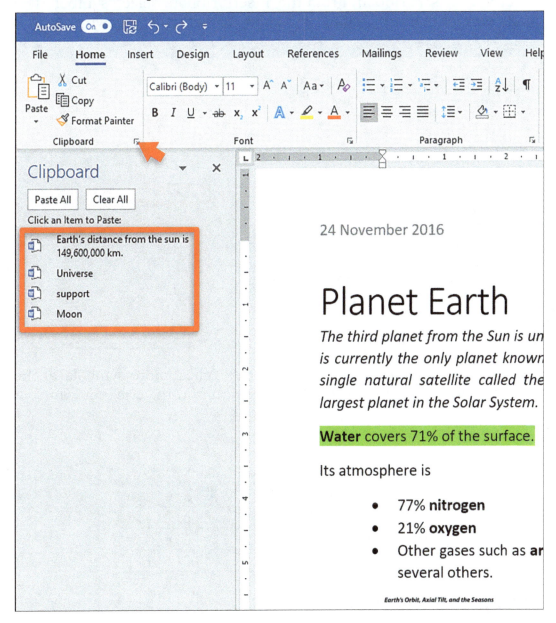

Here you'll see a list of all the parts of the document you've copied or cut. You can click on any of these items on the clipboard to paste into your document. The item will be pasted where your cursor is in your document.

Click 'clear all' to clear the clipboard. Right click on an element and select 'delete' to delete an individual item

Inserting Symbols

First place your cursor in the position you want to insert a symbol.

Select your insert ribbon. From the 'insert' ribbon, select 'symbol'. The most commonly used symbols will show up in the drop down box.

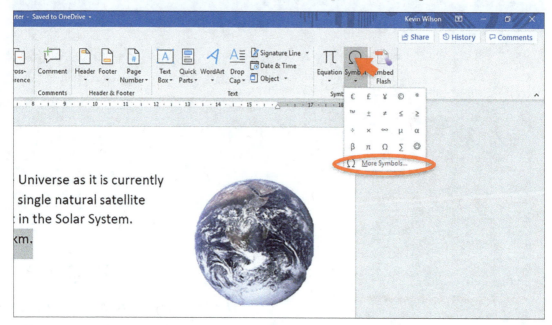

If the symbol you are looking for isn't there, click 'more symbols' at the bottom, and scroll through the list until you find the one you want.

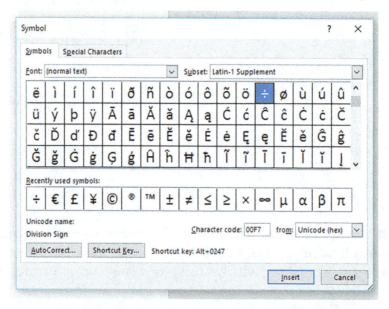

To insert the symbol click on it, then click 'insert'.

The Character Map

The character map is a useful tool to have open if you need to insert symbols.

You can find it if you type in...

`character map`

...into the search field on your task bar.

In the window that appears, you can search for all types of symbols. Select the font typeface from the 'fonts' field, then scroll down all the symbols. When you find the one you want, click on it and click copy.

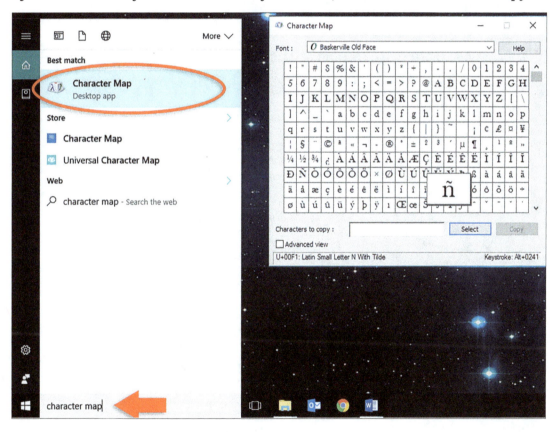

To insert the symbol into your document, open your document in Word, if you haven't already done so.

If your document is open, click the Word icon on your taskbar to switch to Word.

Click the position in the document you want the symbol to appear, go to your home ribbon and click paste.

Hidden Characters

Word also inserts formatting characters such as carriage returns, spaces, tab characters that are hidden by default, to make editing your document easier for you.

To show these characters, click the 'show/hide special characters' icon on the home ribbon.

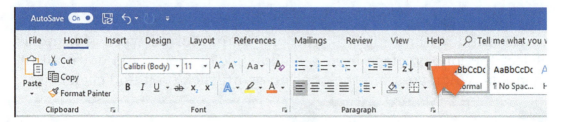

You can see in the screen below, the special characters.

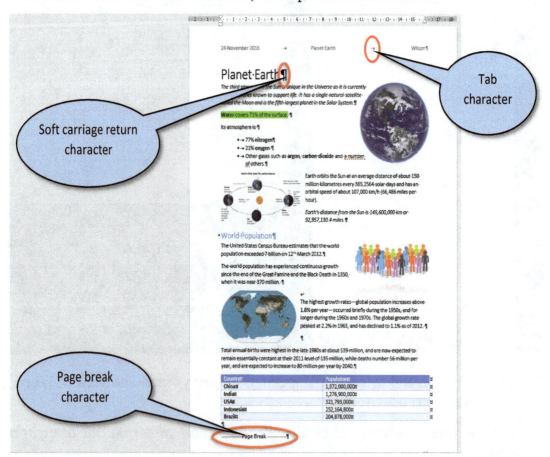

These characters don't print when you print out your document, they are there for formatting purposes.

Equations

Word has built in templates for displaying equations correctly and has some very common ones built in.

$$Speed = \frac{Distance}{Time}$$

$$Volume = \frac{4}{3}\pi r^3$$

You can build equations using the equation tool on the insert ribbon.

If we want to build the second equation first, go to your insert ribbon and click 'equation'

In the box that appears, we can start building the equation.

First type

volume =

Then we need to insert a fraction, so type

4 / 3

Now we need to insert a symbol for Pi. So from the design ribbon, scroll down the list of symbols in the centre, until you find Pi (π). Double click to add.

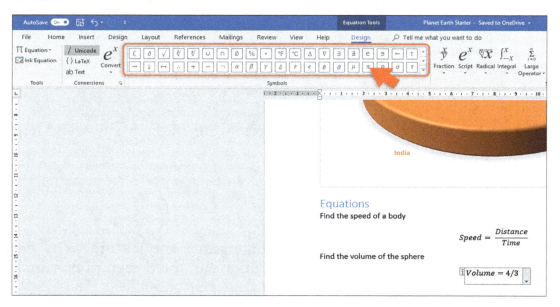

Now click 'script' from the design ribbon and select 'superscript' to add the last part of the equation: r^3

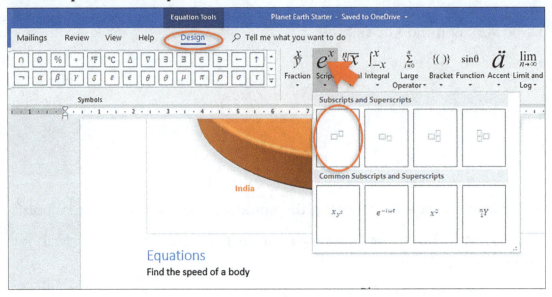

You'll see two little boxes appear on your equation.

Click the bigger box and type:

$$r$$

Then in the smaller box type:

$$3$$

This will give you:

$$r^3$$

Now we have our equation. Note the formatting of the fraction and font styles.

$$Volume = \frac{4}{3}\pi r^3$$

This is a very simple example to demonstrate the feature. Why not experiment with some of the other equations on the design ribbon such as integrals, radicals and functions.

You can also enter equations using LaTeX. To do this select 'equation' from the 'insert' ribbon tab.

Select the LaTeX icon.

Now you can enter your equation. The LaTeX code for the simple equation to evaluate the volume of a cube is

```
V = \frac{{4\pi r^3 }}{3}
```

So we can type this in to the equation box

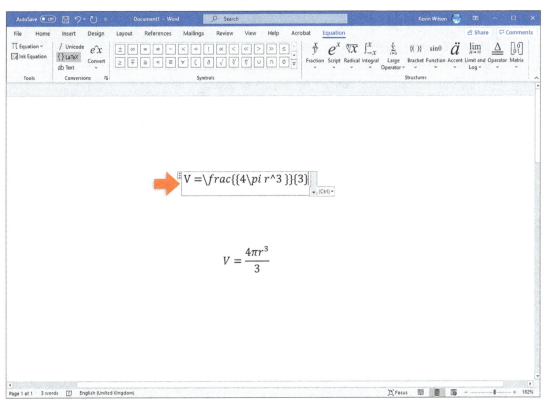

Hit enter on your keyboard and word will automatically format the equation for you.

Headers and Footers

Headers and footers appear at the top and bottom of a page. For example, the header on this page is "Chapter 3: Microsoft Word" and the footer is a page number on the bottom right.

Inserting Headers & Footers

To insert a header, go to your insert ribbon and click 'header'. From the drop down menu, select a header template. The 3 column header is commonly used, allowing you to enter something on the left, center or right of the header.

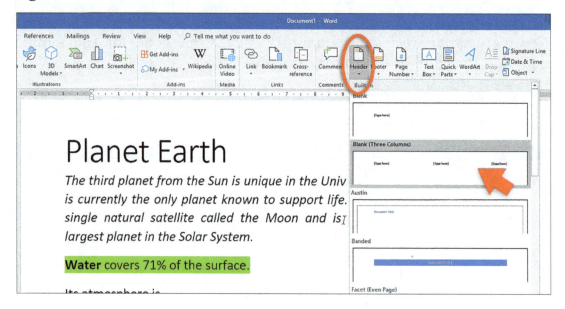

Now fill in the *[type here]* place holders with your information. Double click the place holders to select them, then type your information.

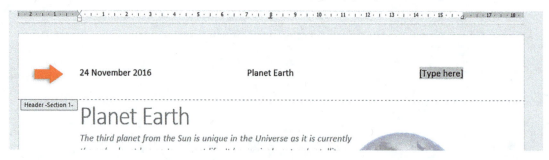

Try inserting a footer. Perhaps a logo on the bottom left? Do the same for inserting a header, except select 'footer' from the insert ribbon. Give it a try.

Editing Headers & Footers

To edit the header, double click in the white space at the top of the document. This is the header space.

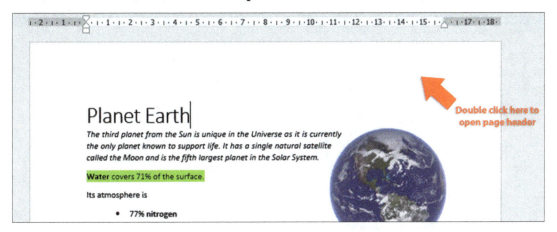

You will see the header & footer design ribbon appear and the header section marked at the top of the document.

You can insert a date & time field, you can even insert a picture or a logo.

To insert pictures, click 'pictures' to insert a picture stored on your computer, or click 'online pictures' to search Bing. Use the same procedure for inserting images into a document.

Try editing the footer of the document.

Page Numbering

Inserting page numbers are similar to inserting footers. To generate page numbers, go to your insert ribbon and click 'page numbers'.

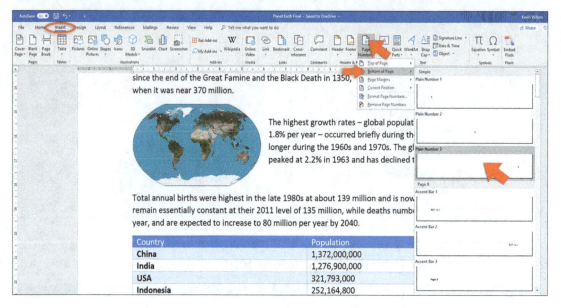

From the drop down menu, select 'bottom of page', which is usually where page numbers are.

From the templates, select 'plain number 3', because we want the page numbers on the bottom right. Similarly if you wanted them in the centre, select 'plain number 2' template.

Why not try some of the other templates, 'accent bar 2' perhaps?

You'll see the page footer open with the page number.

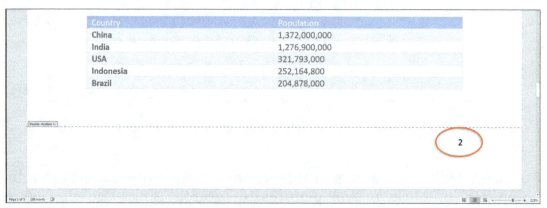

Click 'close header & footer' from the header design ribbon at the top of the screen.

Page Borders

You can add a page border to your documents. To do this, go to your design ribbon and select 'page border'.

From the dialog box that appears, select one of the settings listed down the left hand side. I'm going to select 'shadow'.

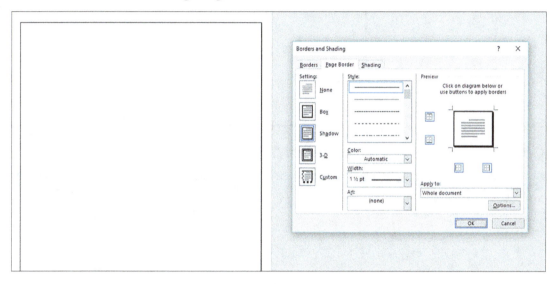

You can adjust the thickness of the lines by adjusting the width.

Or try some border art. Border art as its name suggests allows you to create borders with pre-set clipart images.

Click on the 'art' field and select a design. Since this document is about Earth, I'm going to choose the small planets.

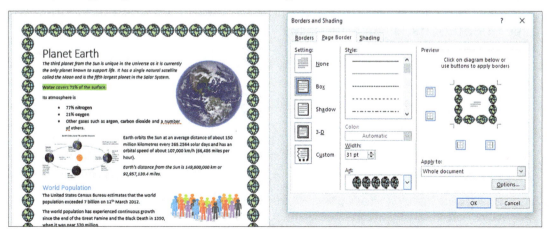

Page & Section Breaks

There may be times where you need to force a new page. Perhaps you are writing a report and you need to start a new chapter or section. Instead of pressing the return key until a new page is created, you should insert a page break.

To do this, make sure you're on the page where the break is to be inserted. Remember breaks are added after the current page.

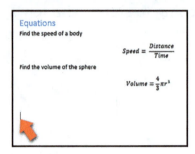

Go to your layout ribbon and click 'breaks'.

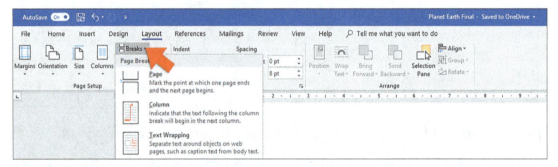

Here you will see a list of different types of breaks. For a simple page break, select the first option, 'page'.

Section breaks divide the document into independent sections. Each section can be formatted independently, meaning you can have different page orientations, sizes and styles.

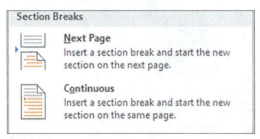

A page break merely forces text to start on a new page of the same section.

Creating Columns

Adding columns to your document arranges your text in a similar fashion to a newspaper.

To do this, go to your layout ribbon and click 'columns'. From the drop down menu, select how many columns you want. In this example, I am going to create a 3 column article.

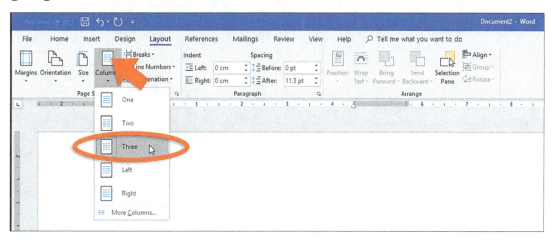

Now, when you start typing your article, Word will arrange your text into columns.

Lorem ipsum dolor sit amet, consectetuer adipiscing elit. Aenean commodo ligula eget dolor. Aenean massa. Cum sociis natoque penatibus et magnis dis parturient montes, nascetur ridiculus mus. Donec quam felis, ultricies nec, pellentesque eu, pretium quis, sem. Nulla consequat massa quis enim. Donec pede justo, fringilla vel, aliquet nec, vulputate eget, arcu. In enim justo, rhoncus ut, imperdiet a, venenatis vitae, justo. Nullam dictum felis eu pede mollis pretium. Integer tincidunt. Cras dapibus.

Vivamus elementum semper nisi. Aenean

orci eget eros faucibus tincidunt. Duis leo. Sed fringilla mauris sit amet nibh. Donec sodales sagittis magna. Sed consequat, leo eget bibendum sodales, augue velit cursus nunc, quis gravida magna mi a libero. Fusce vulputate eleifend sapien.

Vestibulum purus quam, scelerisque ut, mollis sed, nonummy id, metus. Nullam accumsan lorem in dui. Cras ultricies mi eu turpis hendrerit fringilla. Vestibulum ante ipsum primis in faucibus orci luctus et ultrices posuere cubilia Curae; In ac dui quis mi consectetuer lacinia. Nam pretium turpis et arcu.

auctor et, hendrerit quis, nisi. Curabitur ligula sapien, tincidunt non, euismod vitae, posuere imperdiet, leo. Maecenas malesuada. Praesent congue erat at massa. Sed cursus turpis vitae tortor. Donec posuere vulputate arcu. Phasellus accumsan cursus velit. Vestibulum ante ipsum primis in faucibus orci luctus et ultrices posuere cubilia Curae; Sed aliquam, nisi quis porttitor congue, elit erat euismod orci, ac placerat dolor lectus quis orci. Phasellus consectetuer vestibulum elit. Aenean tellus metus, bibendum sed, posuere ac, mattis non, nunc. Vestibulum fringilla pede sit amet augue. In

If you need to adjust the spacing between the columns, from the layout ribbon, click 'columns' then click 'more columns'.

Change the values in the 'width and spacing' section below.

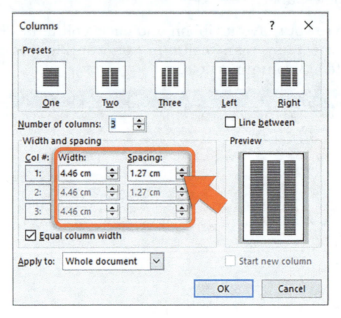

This is what the columns will look like. You can see the column width and column spacing marked on the image below, according to the settings in the dialog box.

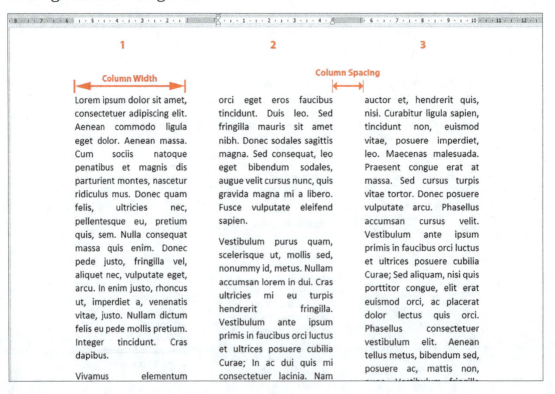

Watermarks

You can add watermarks such as 'confidential', or 'draft' to your documents. To do this, go to your design ribbon and click 'watermark'. From the drop down, select one of the templates.

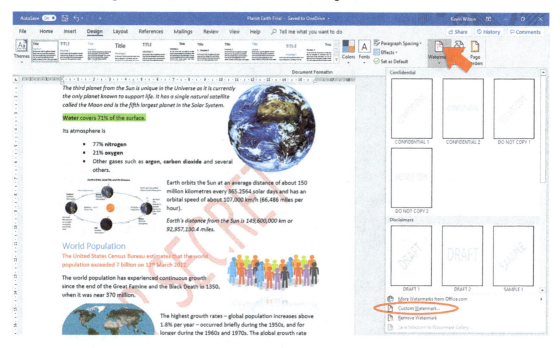

You can also create your own. What if my document was top secret? To do this, click 'custom water mark' from the drop down menu.

Enter your text, 'TOP SECRET' in to the text field. Change the color to red. Click 'ok' when you're done.

Cover Pages

You can add pre-designed cover pages to your documents. These work well if you are submitting a sales report, a manuscript or something that needs a title page.

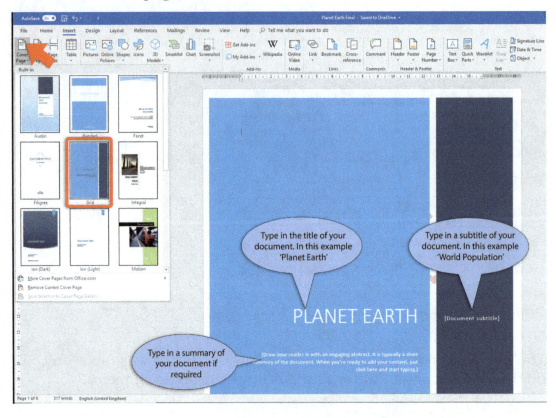

This cover page is looking a bit boring, so I'm going to add an image. For this example, I am going to add an image of the planet earth.

First go to your insert ribbon and click 'online pictures'.

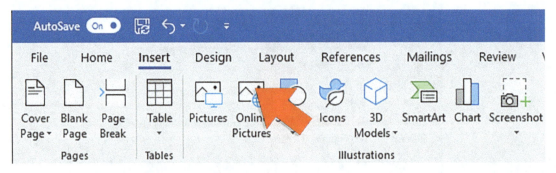

If you want to insert a picture of your own, select 'pictures' instead of 'online pictures', then select the picture you want to insert from the dialog box.

From the dialog box that appears, type what you're looking for into the Bing search, in this example I'm going to type 'earth'.

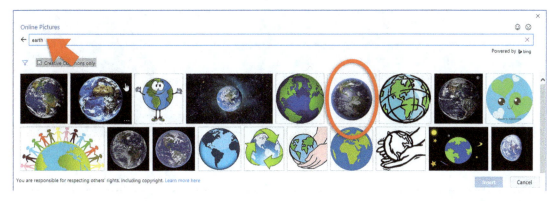

From the list of images that appear, I want one that will blend well with the transparent background. The one circled above works well. Click on it then click 'insert'.

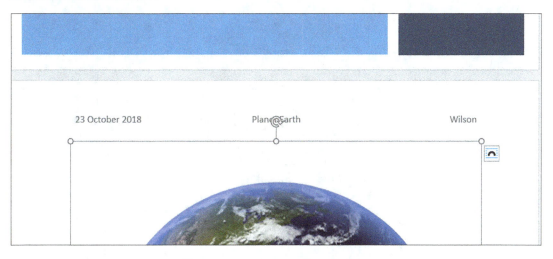

Now the problem is, Word has inserted the image but it isn't in the right place, also the image might be behind something else. First we need to make the image float. To do this, click the image you just inserted, go to the format ribbon and select 'wrap text'. From the drop down, select 'in front of text'.

Now click and drag the image into position on your cover page. Drag your image onto the cover page if needed.

Use the resize handles circled in the illustration above, to resize your image.

Drag the image into a position that looks good, as shown in the example above.

Contents Pages

The contents tool works by scanning your document for heading styles. For example, Title, Heading 1, Heading 2, Heading 3 and so on.

To add an automatic table of contents, go to your 'references' ribbon menu and select 'automatic table 2'. This option will scan your document for 'heading 1', 'heading 2' and 'heading 3' styles and add them to the table.

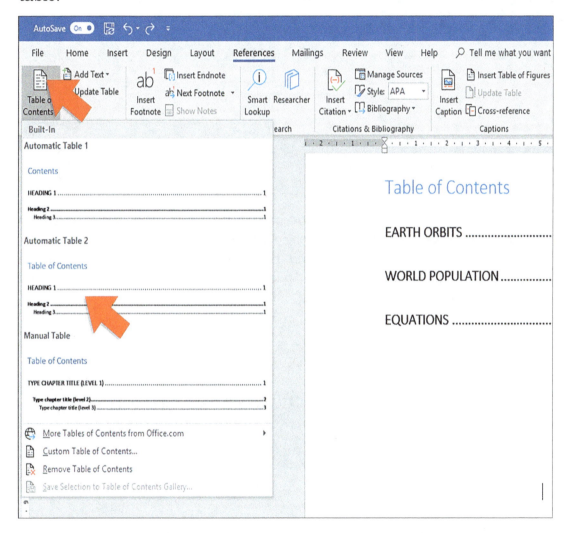

You may notice that in our document we have used a title style which has not been picked up by the table of contents generator.

If you have used styles other than 'heading 1', 'heading 2' and 'heading 3', they won't get picked up.

Remember, we used the 'title' style for the title of our document.

To create a table of contents with other styles, you will need to select 'custom table of contents' from the drop down menu. Then from the dialog box, select 'options'.

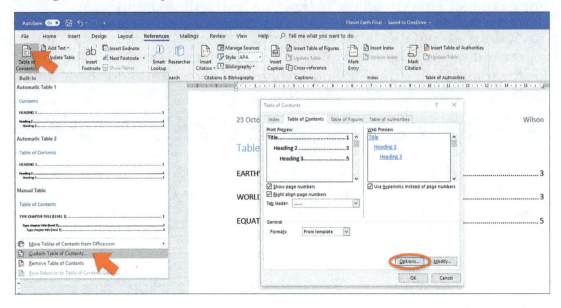

Now in the box that appears, you need to put the heading styles in the order you want them to appear in the table of contents. So in our example document, we have used the 'Title' style for all the chapter headings, so this one needs to appear first, so we scroll down the list until we see the 'Title' style. Enter 1 in the box next to it.

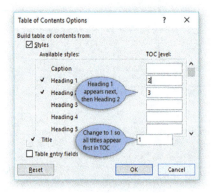

Next we have used Heading 1 for all the subtitles. So again in the list we look for heading 1 style. We want this one to appear second, so enter 2 in the box next to it.

We used Heading 2 for all the sections and we want these included. So find heading 2 in the list and enter 3 in the box next to it.

Click OK when you're done and Word will generate your table of contents.

Indexes

Select the text you want to flag as an index entry. Go to your references ribbon and click 'Mark Entry'.

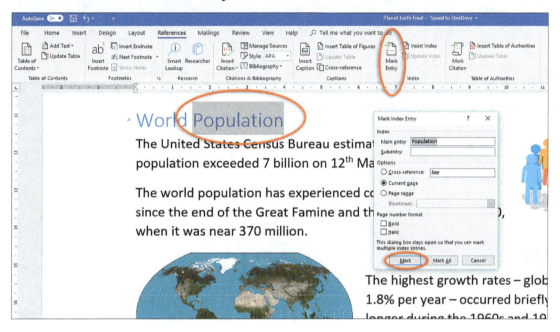

Click 'mark' to mark only that particular occurrence of the word, click 'mark all' to mark every occurrence of the word in your document. Do this with all the words you want to appear in your index - use titles and keywords.

You can have an index that just runs down the left of the page. This is a single column index. You can increase the number of columns for your index. This helps to save space on your page if you are writing long documents. Here's a three column index.

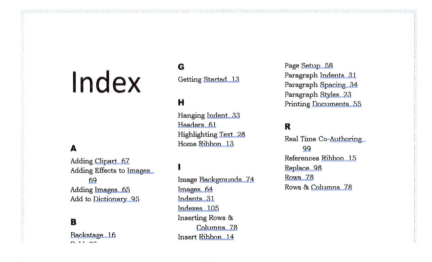

To generate an index, it's a good idea to first insert a blank page or a page break. Click at the top of the page (this is where the index will start). Now from the references ribbon, click 'Insert Index'.

Choose a type: indented or run-in. In an indented style, main headings are followed by indented subheadings, each on its own line. In run-in style, subheadings follow main headings continuously, separated by commas.

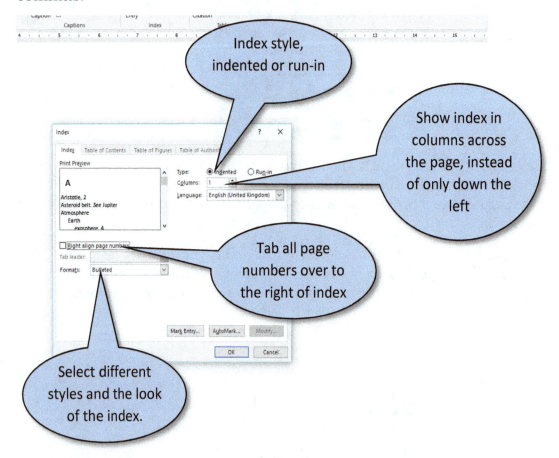

Then specify the number of columns to span the index across.

You can also choose a format if you select the format drop down menu, and select an option. In this example, I am using a 'bulleted' format.

Click OK when you're done.

Search & Replace

You can search for any word in your document by clicking the 'find' icon on the home ribbon

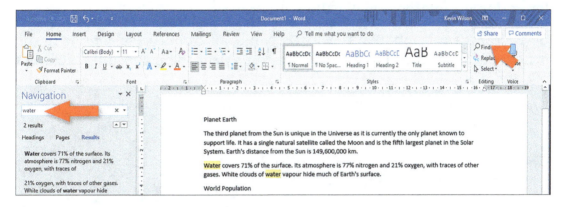

On the side bar that opens up, type the word or phrase you want to search for. In this example, I am searching for the word 'water'. You will see Word has highlighted the words it has found in yellow.

You can also replace a word or phrase. To do this click 'replace' on the home ribbon. In this document, if I wanted to replace all the words 'universe' with 'galaxy'. I'd type in 'universe' in the 'find what' field, and 'galaxy' in the 'replace with' field.

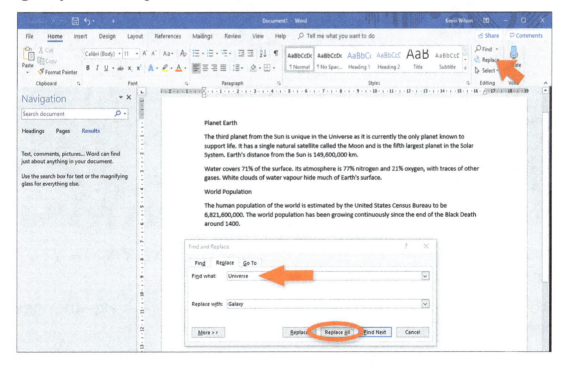

Click 'replace all' to change all the instances of the word.

Pen Support

In Microsoft Word, you'll see an additional ribbon menu called 'draw'. This has all your drawing tools such as pens, highlighters and an eraser for you to annotate your Word documents.

Select the 'draw' ribbon and select a pen color from the selections in the centre of the ribbon. From here you can select the color and thickness of your pen.

With these tools, you can draw directly onto your Word document, as shown above.

This means you can label diagrams, handwrite notes, make drawings and so on, all using your stylus or finger on your tablet.

You will then be able to save the document including all the annotations or drawings you have made.

Here you can highlight and annotate a typed Word document directly on your tablet using your stylus pen.

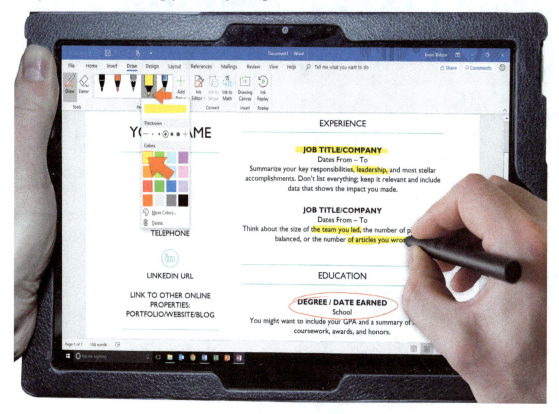

You can then save the document with all the annotations and highlights as well as share these with colleagues or friends.

Either use the share icon on the top right of your screen, or you can email the document over.

Adding Graphics

In this chapter, we'll explore how to add graphics and images. We'll look at:

- Adding Images
- Insert from a File
- Stock Images
- Online Pictures
- Download and Insert from Google Images
- Adding Effects to Images
- Formatting Images
- Rotate Images
- Wrap Text around Images
- Remove Image Backgrounds
- SmartArt
- WordArt

To help you better understand this section, take a look at the video resources. Open your web browser and navigate to the following website:

elluminetpress.com/word-img

You'll also need to download the source files from:

elluminetpress.com/word

Adding Images

Adding images to your document is straightforward. There are three ways:

- Your own photos and pictures stored on your computer or OneDrive.

- Online. From Bing images.

- Stock Photos. This is a large library of images that can be used in your documents.

Click on the line in your document where you want your photograph or image to appear.

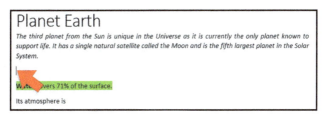

Insert from a File

Go to your insert ribbon and click on 'Pictures'. Select 'from device'.

Choose the picture or photo you want from the dialog box that appears. Click insert.

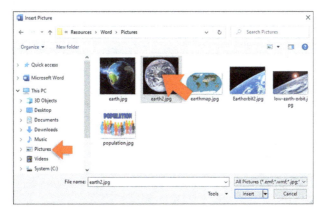

This will insert your photo into your document.

Stock Images

Microsoft have recently added royalty free stock images to their library. To add a stock image, go to the insert ribbon and click 'pictures'. Select 'stock images'.

Here you can download all sorts of stock images. Along the top of the window you'll see some categories.

Stock images contains a general image library you can search. Icons contains small pictures and symbols you can use to illustrate different ideas in your documents.

Cutout people is a library of people shot against a transparent background meaning you can insert them into your document without a background.

Stickers are little characters you can insert into your work.

Search for an image, click the image in the search results then click 'insert'.

Online Pictures

To add an online image from Bing Images, go to the insert ribbon and click 'pictures'. Select 'online images'.

Select or search for the image you want to add. Eg I'm searching for an image to illustrate 'world population' in my document

Select the image you want, click insert.

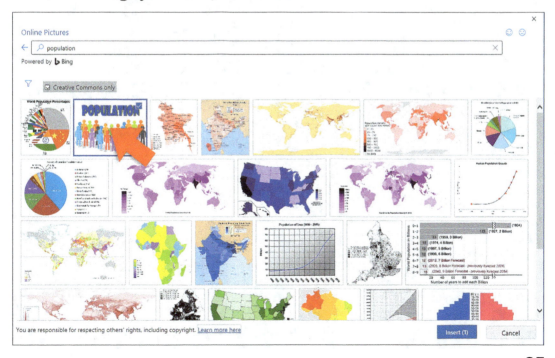

Download and Insert from Google Images

You can also search for images on Google. When you download an image, make sure you save them into your pictures folder. Open your web browser and run a google search, then select 'images'.

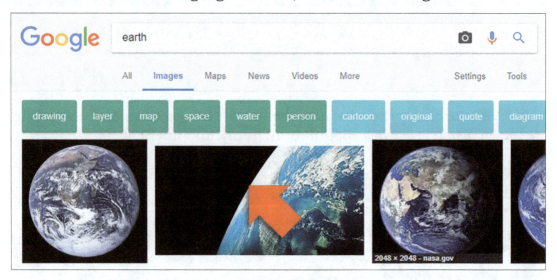

Click on the image thumbnail in the search results to view the full size image. Then right click image, select 'save image as' from the popup menu.

From the dialog box that appears, save the picture into your 'pictures' folder either on your PC or OneDrive folder.

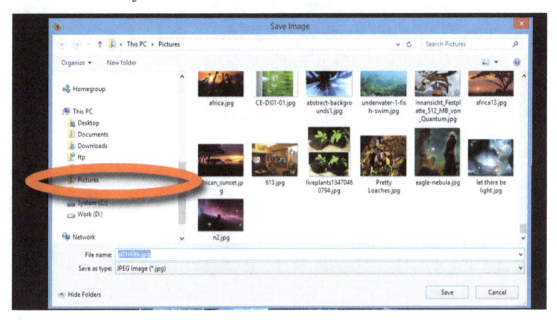

Once your image is saved into your pictures folder, you can import them into your Word document using the same procedure at the beginning of the chapter.

Once imported into Word, you may need to resize the image, as sometimes they can come in a bit big. To do this click on the image, you'll see small handles appear on each corner of the image.

These are called resize handles. You can use them by clicking and dragging a corner toward the centre of the image to make it smaller as shown below. Hold down the shift key as you resize the image to prevent it from being distorted.

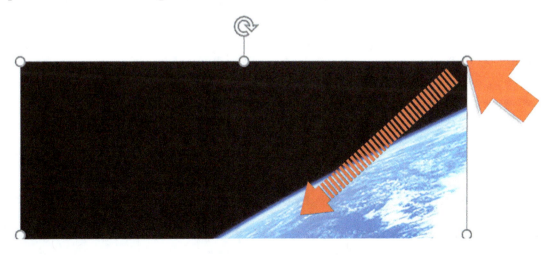

Adding Effects to Images

To add effects to your images, such as shadows and borders, click on your image, then select the Format ribbon.

In this example, click on the population image.

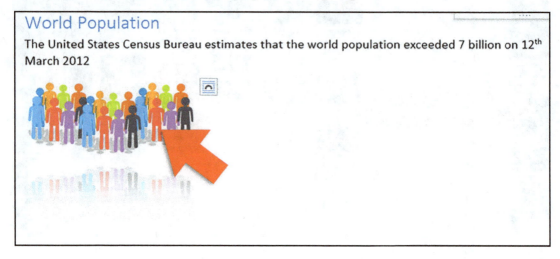

I want to create a nice reflection style to the image. To do this, click 'picture effects', then go down to 'reflection'. Select a variation as shown below.

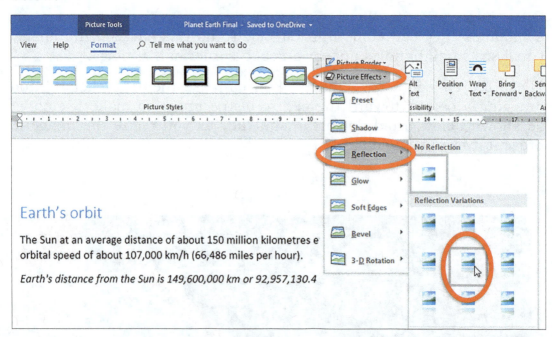

Try different effects, such as 'shadow', 'bevel' or 'glow'.

See what effect they have...

Format Image

Formatting pictures in Microsoft Word allows you to enhance the visual appeal and clarity of your images. You can adjust the size, color, effects, and other aspects of your pictures

Right-click on the picture in your Word document. From the popup menu select 'format picture'.

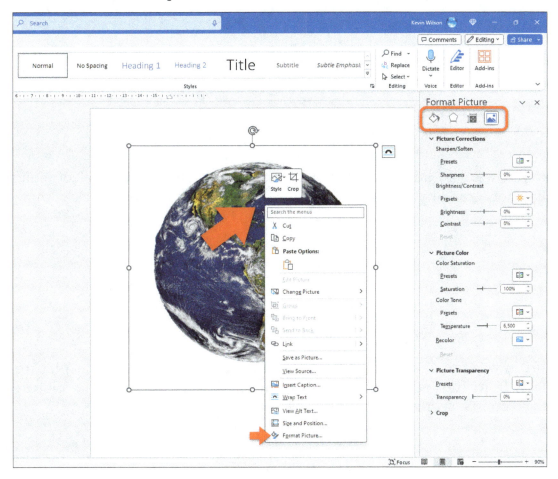

In the 'format picture' pane on the right hand side, you will see four tabs along the top. Let's take a look at what tools each tab contains.

- **Fill & Line:** adjust the fill options of the picture, such as solid fill, gradient fill, picture or texture. Adjust the border and lines.
- **Effects:** modify shadows, reflections, glow and other artistic effects.
- **Layout & Properties:** choose text wrap, image position, size, and other properties such as alt text.
- **Picture:** adjust brightness, color, image compression, or replace the picture with another.

For example, if you want to change the fill background, select 'fill and line'. Under the fill section, select the effect you want, eg gradient fill. Adjust the settings that appear according to the effect you want to add.

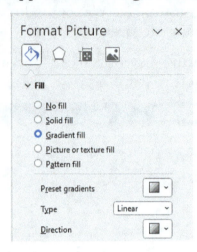

If you want to add a border, click the 'line section', then select 'solid line', or 'gradient line' etc. Also select the color of the line.

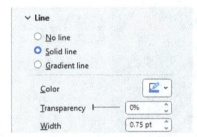

If you want to change the effects on the image itself, select the 'picture' icon from the four tabs along the top of the pane. Open the 'picture corrections' section and adjust the settings.

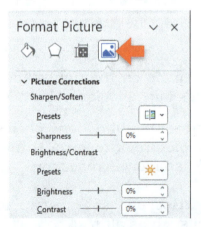

Also try 'picture color' to change the color hue of the image. Experiment with some of the settings to see how they affect the image.

Cropping Images

If you insert an image into your document, and it has unwanted parts, or you want to concentrate on one particular piece of the picture, you can crop the image

First, insert an image from your pictures library into your document.

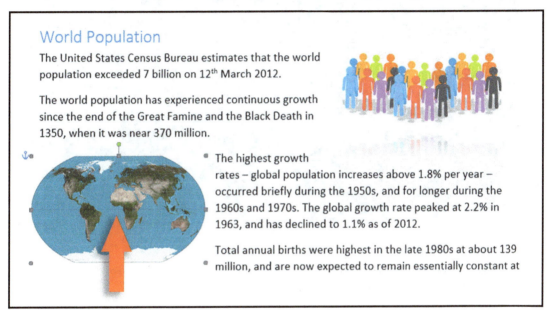

To crop, click on the image, then click the format ribbon. From the format ribbon, click the crop icon.

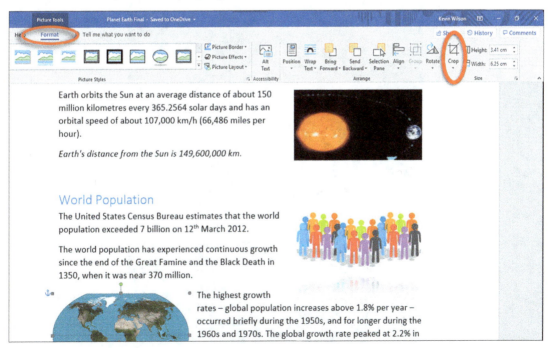

Chapter 4: Adding Graphics

If you look closely at your image, you will see crop handles around the edges, shown circled below.

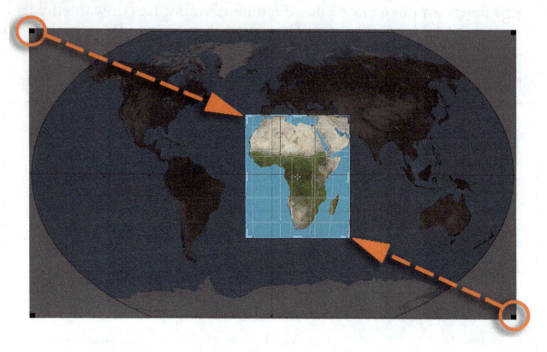

Click and drag these handles around the part of the image you want to keep. Eg, I just want to show Africa in the image.

The dark grey bits will be removed to leave the bit of the image inside the crop square.

Wrap Text Around Images

When you insert an image, the image will be inserted in-line with text, meaning the image will show on one line, with text both above and below.

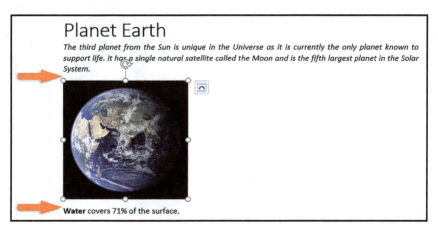

The document would flow much better if you wrapped the relevant text around the image. To change the text wrap, click on the image and from the format ribbon, click 'text wrap'. Select 'square' from the drop down list to align the text squarely around the border of the image.

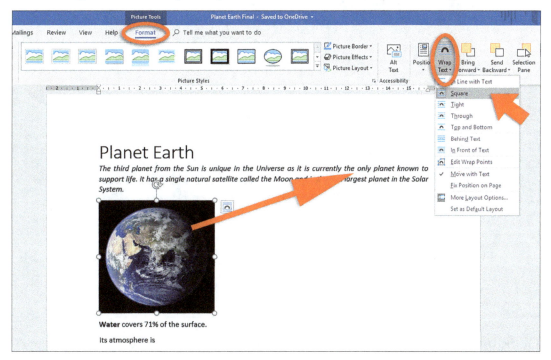

Click and drag the image into position. As you do this, you'll notice the text will arrange itself around the image.

This image, I will align top right, in line with the first paragraph.

If your image has a white background or isn't square, you can wrap your text around the actual image.

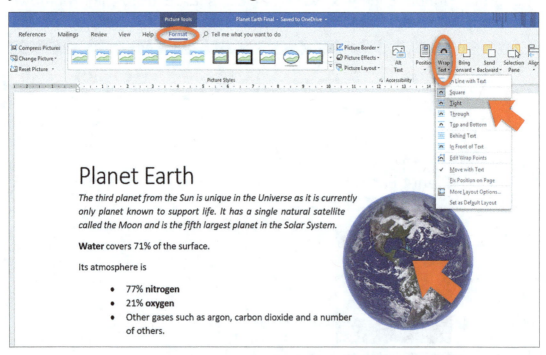

Click on the image and select your format ribbon. Click on 'wrap text' from the drop down menu, and select 'tight'.

Try some of the other text wraps. What happens when you select 'through' or 'behind text'?

Rotate an Image

Click on the image you want to rotate. When the image is selected, you'll see small square handles around its edges, indicating that it's active. At the top of the selected image, you'll see a rotate handle in the middle. Click and drag this handle to the left or right. You'll see the image rotate.

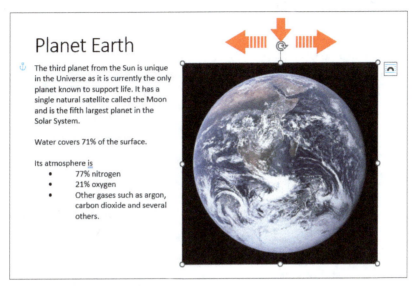

If you want to rotate the image to a specific number of degrees, first click on the image to select it. Select the 'format picture' ribbon tab, then click on 'rotate'. From the drop down select 'more rotation options'.

In the dialog box, select the 'size' tab, go down to the 'rotate' section. Enter the number of degrees to rotate in the field.

Remove Image Backgrounds

If your image has a solid color background, you can remove it to make it transparent. This can help to blend your image into your document.

Take the example of the image of the planet earth, if you look at it, the image has a black background. This doesn't particularly blend well with the rest of the document.

To remove the black, click the image and select your format ribbon. Click 'remove background'.

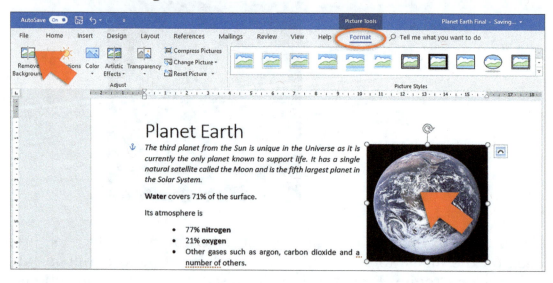

You'll notice a white box with stretch handles appear around your image.

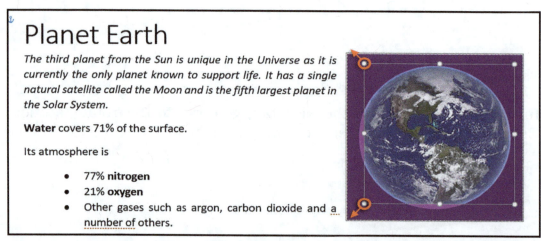

Stretch the box by clicking and dragging the handles outwards until the purple area surrounds the image, and there is no purple spilling over into the image.

The purple bit is a mask, and highlights the bit of the image that will be removed, or 'masked out'.

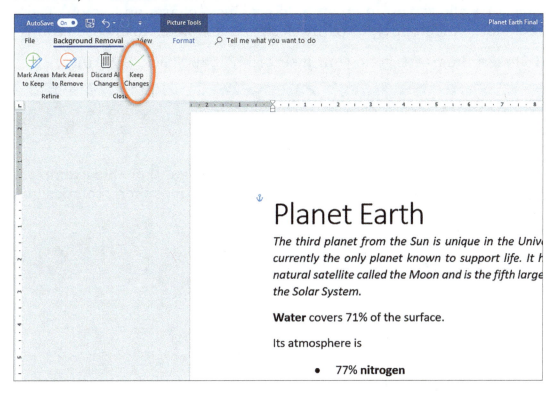

Once you have done that, click 'keep changes' on the top left of your screen.

You'll see that all the black surrounding the image has been removed, and the image blends in a lot better with the text.

You might want to resize the image and reposition it.

SmartArt

SmartArt allows you to create info graphics, charts and so on. There are a lot of different types of pre-designed templates to choose from.

To insert SmartArt, go to your insert ribbon and click 'SmartArt'.

From the dialog box that appears, select a design. For this example, I am going to select 'picture strips' to display my atmospheric composition data in our document.

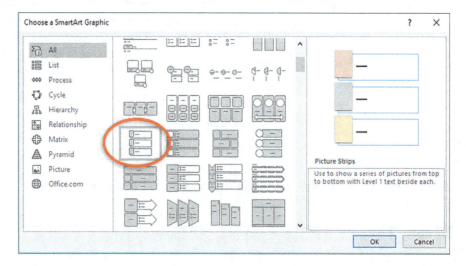

To edit the information, click in the place holders to enter your own data.

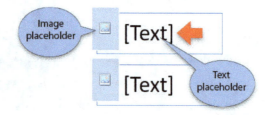

If you want to add a bullet point, select 'add bullet' from the 'SmartArt Design' ribbon

Here I've added a bullet point under the title

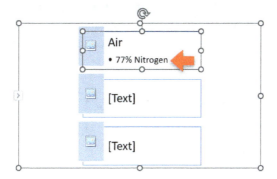

If you need to add another shape, select the shape where you want to add another, then from the 'SmartArt Design ribbon' click 'add shape'. Select 'add after'.

Click 'text pane' to reveal the text pane. The text pane provides a convenient way to enter and edit text for the shapes within the graphic. Just click on the text and image place holders to add your own content.

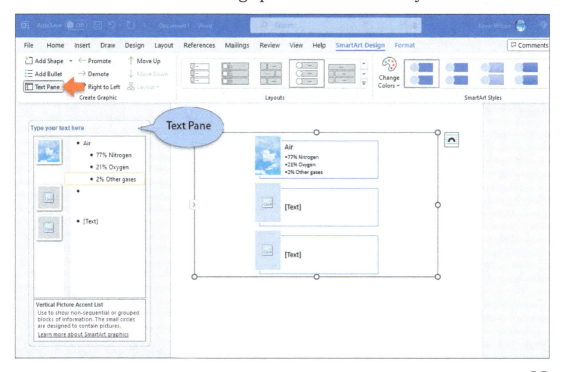

In this particular graphic, you can add images to each of the sections. To do this, double click on the image place holder. To search for images on line, select 'online pictures' from the options.

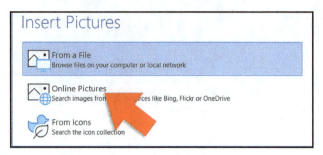

From the dialog box that appears, enter your search term. In this example, the next section is about water, so I'd type water into the search field.

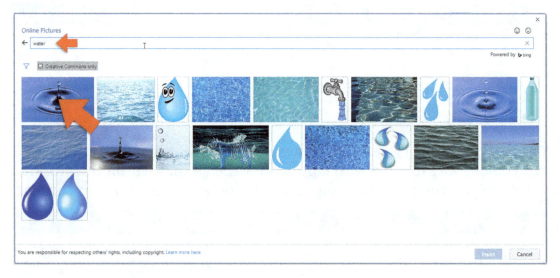

From the search results, select an image that you think best represents 'water'. Click 'insert', to insert the image into the place holder.

Do the same for the other images.

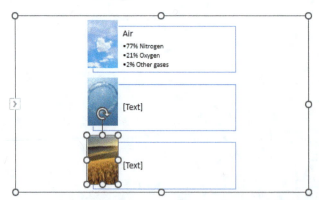

You can also change the design of the graphic. To do this, click on the SmartArt graphic and select the ' Smart Art design' ribbon. Click the 'change color' icon, then select a scheme from the drop down menu.

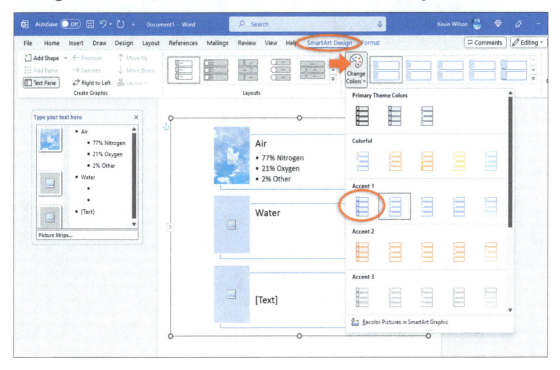

You can also change the style. To do this, select one of the styles in the 'SmartArt style' section of the 'SmartArt Design' ribbon.

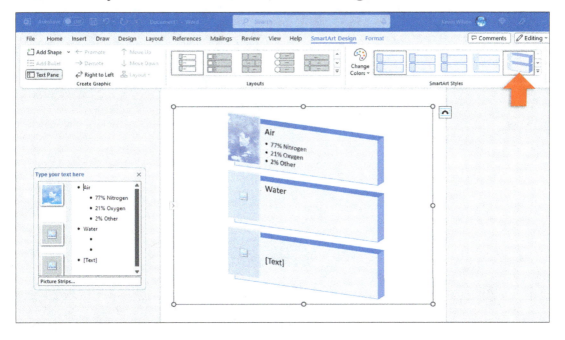

Perhaps a 3D version of your graphic?

You can also change the layout, if you prefer to use a different one to the one you initially selected. To do this, click the small down arrow to the right of layouts section on the 'SmartArt design' ribbon.

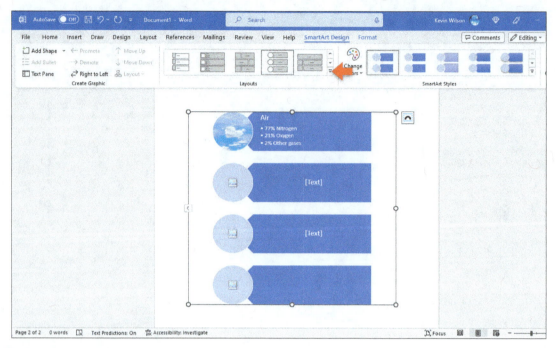

Select a layout from the list.

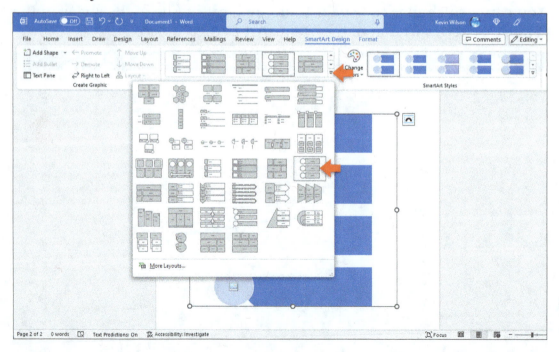

Experiment with some of the other layouts and themes to see how they affect the SmartArt object.

WordArt

WordArt is useful for creating headings and titles. To add wordart, select your 'insert' ribbon tab and click the wordart icon. Select a style from the drop down menu.

From the 'shape format' ribbon tab you can format your wordart text. To do this, use the 'wordart styles' section.

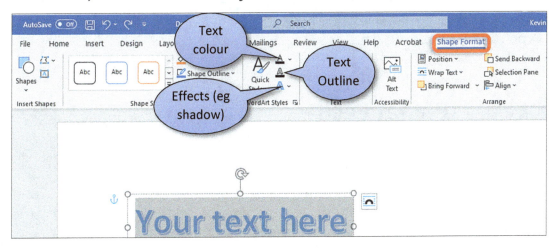

Now you can customise the text. If you want to change the text color, click the text color icon, select a color from the pallet. Similarly if you want to change the outline, click the text outline icon, select a color from the pallet.

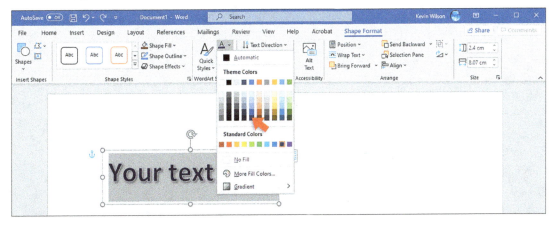

Chapter 4: Adding Graphics

If you want to add an effect such as a glow or shadow, click the effects icon, browse through the drop down menu and select an effect to apply.

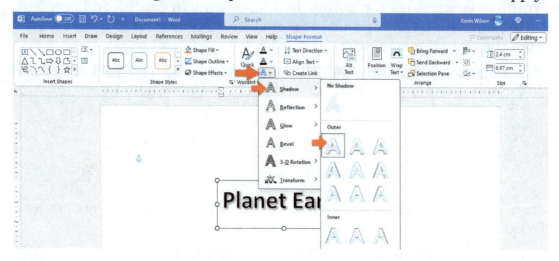

Type in your heading or title.

You can apply transformations to the WordArt. Transformation alter the shape and orientation of text to create visually distinctive and appealing titles or headings, but use them sparingly.

Click on the effects icon on the 'shape format' ribbon tab. Go down to 'transform', then select an effect.

Shapes

Shapes serve multiple purposes. They can enhance both the aesthetic and functional aspects of a document.

To insert a shape, go to the 'insert' ribbon tab. Click on the 'shapes' icon. You can select from a variety of shapes such as lines, rectangles, circles, arrows, callouts, and many more. Click on one to select it.

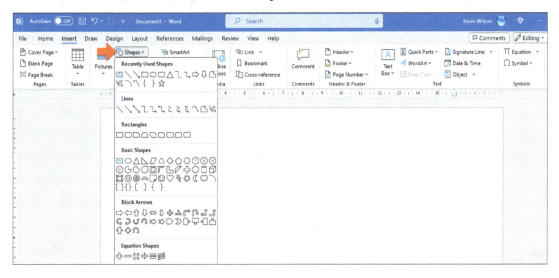

To add the shape to your document, click then drag your mouse pointer to set the size of the shape.

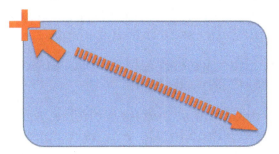

Once a shape is inserted, click on it, you'll see a 'shape format' ribbon tab appear. To change the shape color, click 'shape fill' then select a color. Similarly to change the outline color and thickness, click 'shape outline'. To change the outline color select a color. To change the thickness click 'shape outline', then click 'weight' - select a size.

You can resize a shape by dragging the resize handles that appear around the edge of the selected shape. Or you can rotate the image using the rotate handle. On some shapes, such as rounded rectangles or stars, you'll find yellow adjustment handles. Dragging these handles will alter the characteristics of the shape, for example the roundness of the corners or the length of the star's points and so on.

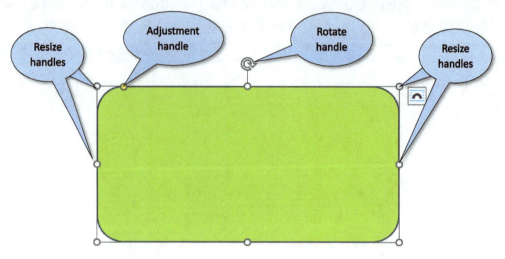

Creating Diagrams

Diagrams are visual representations used to illustrate processes, systems, or ideas in a structured and easily understandable manner. You can use shapes to create various types of diagrams. Imagine a flowchart for a simple process of making a coffee:

For the start of the chart we can add an oval shape. Right click on the shape, select 'add text'. Type in 'Start'.

Next, we can add a diamond shape for a choice. Again right click on the shape, select 'add text'. Type in 'Do you have coffee beans?'.

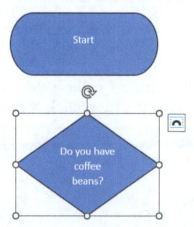

To join the shapes, go up to the 'insert' ribbon tab, click on 'shapes'. From the drop down menu, select a line.

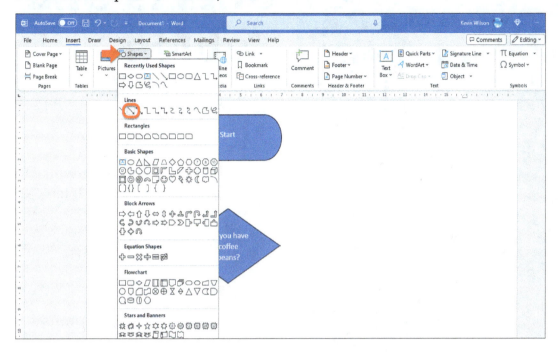

Now draw a line from the 'start' shape to the 'diamond' shape.

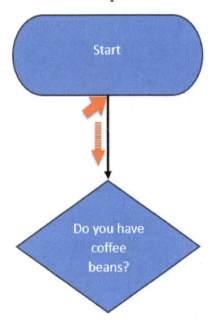

You can change the thickness of the line. To do this, click on the line. Go to the 'shape format' ribbon tab. Click 'shape outline' then select a 'weight'. If you want to change the color, select a color from the pallet.

Have a look at diagrams.docx

5

Charts and Tables

In this chapter, we'll explore how to add tables and charts. We'll look at:

- Adding Tables
- Formatting Tables
- Cell Borders
- Add a Column
- Insert a Row
- Resizing Rows & Columns
- Merge Cells
- Align Cell Text
- Text Direction
- Adding a Chart
- Chart Elements
- Chart Styles
- Data Filters

To help you better understand this section, take a look at the video resources. Open your web browser and navigate to the following website:

elluminetpress.com/word-tab

You'll also need to download the source files from:

elluminetpress.com/word

Adding Tables

We have added some more text about world population to our document. Now we want to add a table to illustrate our text.

To insert a table click on your document where you want the table to appear. In this example, I want it to appear just below world population paragraph.   Go to your insert ribbon and select table.

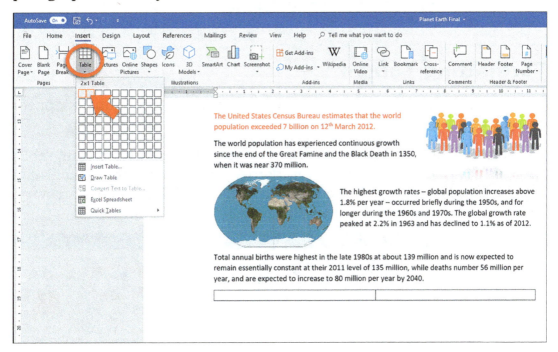

In the grid that appears highlight the number of rows and columns you want. For this table, 1 row and 2 columns.

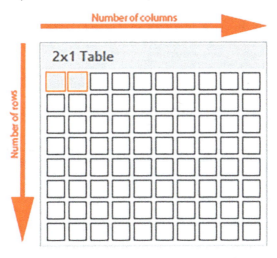

This will add a table with 1 row & 2 columns to your document.

Now just fill in the table. To move between cells on the table press the tab key. When you get to the end of the row, pressing tab will insert a new row.

Country	Population
China	1,372,000,000
India	1,276,900,000
USA	321,793,000
Indonesia	252,164,800
Brazil	204,878,000

Formatting Tables

When you click on a table in your document, two new ribbons appear under 'table tools': design and layout.

The design ribbon allows you to select pre-set designs for your table, such as column and row shading, borders, and color. In the centre of your design ribbon, you'll see a list of designs. Click the small arrow on the bottom right of the 'table styles' panel to open it up.

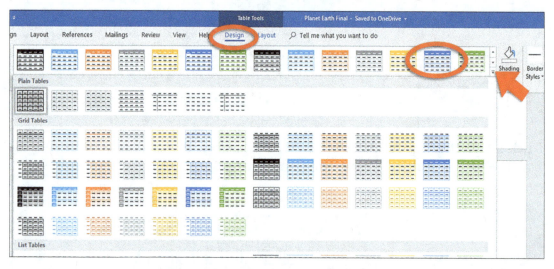

For this table, I am going to choose one with blue headings and shaded rows.

Country	Population
China	1,372,000,000
India	1,276,900,000
USA	321,793,000
Indonesia	252,164,800
Brazil	204,878,000

Cell Borders

Select the cells in the table you want to format. In this case, I want to add a thicker border between the columns 'country' and 'population'. First select the cells, then from the 'table design' ribbon tab, select the thickness of the border.

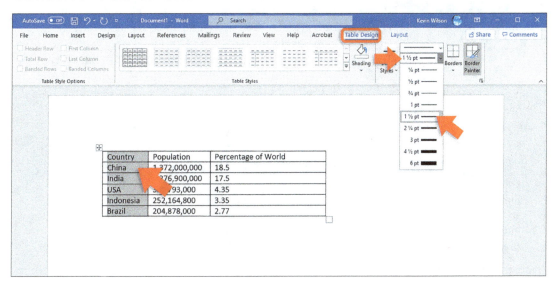

Now select which side of the selected cells you want the border to appear. In this case on the right hand side.

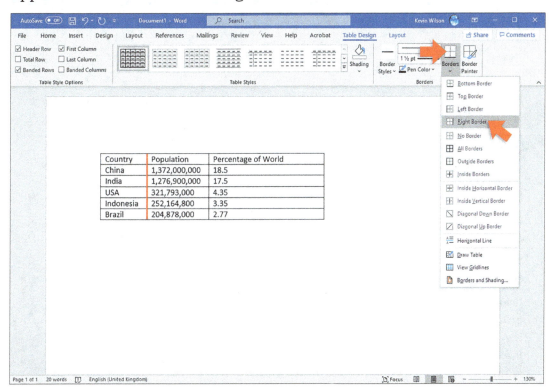

Add a Column

You can add a column to the right hand side of the table. To do this, click in the end column.

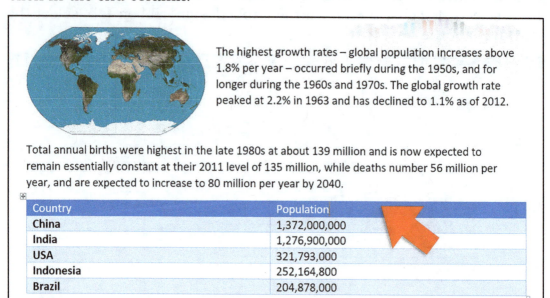

Select the layout ribbon under 'table tools', and select 'insert right'.

This inserts a column to the right of the one you selected.

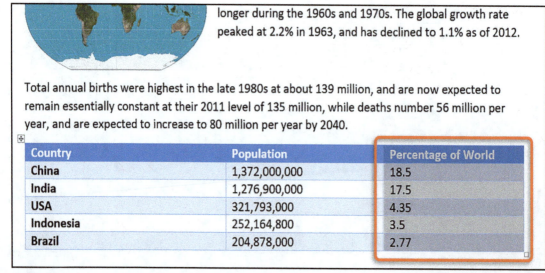

Insert a Row

To add a row, click on the row where you want to insert. For example, I want to add a row between USA and Indonesia. So click on Indonesia, as shown below.

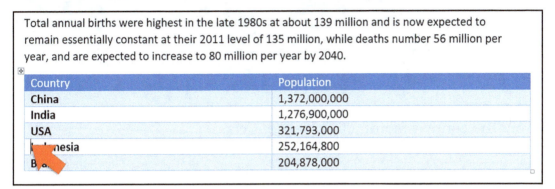

Total annual births were highest in the late 1980s at about 139 million and is now expected to remain essentially constant at their 2011 level of 135 million, while deaths number 56 million per year, and are expected to increase to 80 million per year by 2040.

Country	Population
China	1,372,000,000
India	1,276,900,000
USA	321,793,000
Indonesia	252,164,800
Brazil	204,878,000

Select the layout ribbon from the table tools section.

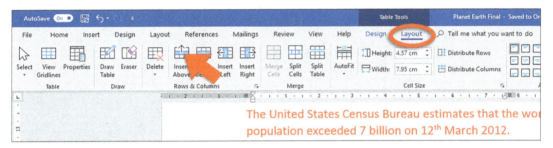

The United States Census Bureau estimates that the world population exceeded 7 billion on 12th March 2012.

Click 'insert above'. This will insert a row above the one you selected earlier.

The highest growth rates – global population increases above 1.8% per year – occurred briefly during the 1950s, and for longer during the 1960s and 1970s. The global growth rate peaked at 2.2% in 1963 and has declined to 1.1% as of 2012.

Total annual births were highest in the late 1980s at about 139 million and is now expected to remain essentially constant at their 2011 level of 135 million, while deaths number 56 million per year, and are expected to increase to 80 million per year by 2040.

Country	Population
China	1,372,000,000
India	1,276,900,000
USA	321,793,000
Indonesia	252,164,800
Brazil	204,878,000

Delete Row

Right-click on the row you want to delete to open the context menu.

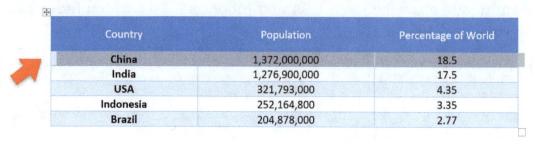

From the context menu, click 'delete rows'.

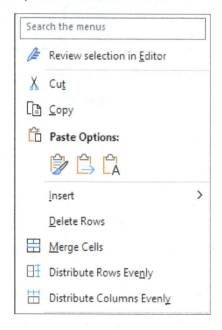

Delete Column

Hover your mouse pointer over the top line of the column you want to delete. You'll see your mouse pointer turn into a small back arrow.

Country	Population	Percentage of World
China	1,372,000,000	18.5
India	1,276,900,000	17.5
USA	321,793,000	4.35
Indonesia	252,164,800	3.35
Brazil	204,878,000	2.77

Right click to reveal the context menu. Select 'delete columns'.

Delete Cell

Right-click inside the cell you want to delete to reveal the context menu. Select 'delete cells'.

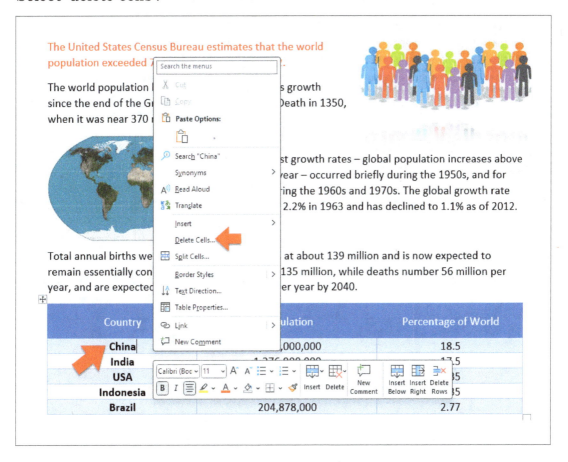

Choose from these options "shift cells left" and "shift cells up".

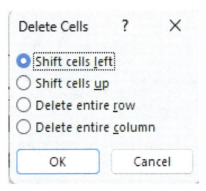

When you select "shift cells left", the cells to the immediate right move left to occupy the position of the deleted cell. When you select "shift cells up" the cell immediately below the deleted cell move up to occupy the space of the deleted cell.

Resizing Rows & Columns

You can resize the column or row by clicking and dragging the row or column dividing line to the size you want.

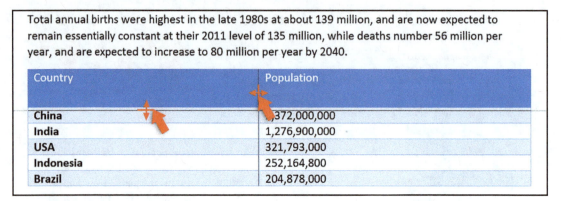

Merge Cells

You can merge cells together. To do this, select the cells you want to merge.

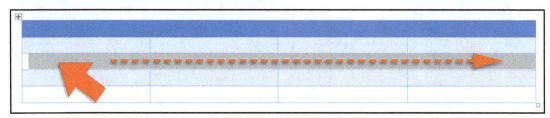

Then select 'merge cells' from the layout ribbon in the table tools section.

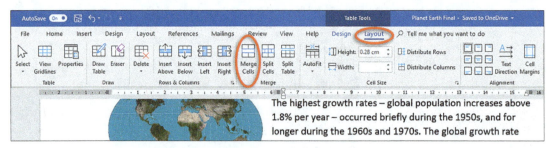

All the selected cells will be merged into a single cell.

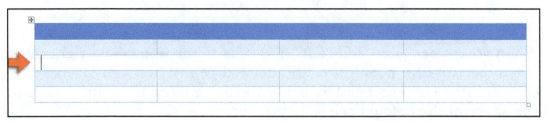

Align Cell Text

You can change text alignment in the cells of the table. To do this, select the cells you want to align. Click and drag...

Country	Population	Percentage of World
China	1,372,000,000	18.5
India	1,276,900,000	17.5
USA	321,793,000	4.35

Select the layout ribbon in the table tools section, as shown below.

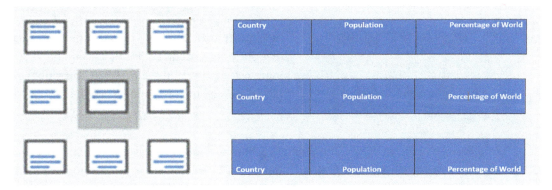

From the alignment section, use the nine boxes to select the text alignment you want to apply to the cells.

Here's a quick guide to what the 9 different alignments look like. In the diagram below, note where each box on the left puts the text in the cells in the example on the right.

For example, select the center box to align the cells to the middle of the cell.

Country	Population	Percentage of World
China	1,372,000,000	18.5
India	1,276,900,000	17.5
USA	321,793,000	4.35
Indonesia	252,164,800	3.35
Brazil	204,878,000	2.77

Text Direction

Also you can arrange the text vertically, this usually works for headings.

To do this, select the heading rows in your table.

Country	Population	Percentage of World
China	1,372,000,000	18.5
India	1,276,900,000	17.5
USA	321,793,000	4.35
Indonesia	252,164,800	3.35
Brazil	204,878,000	2.77

From the layout ribbon click 'text direction'.

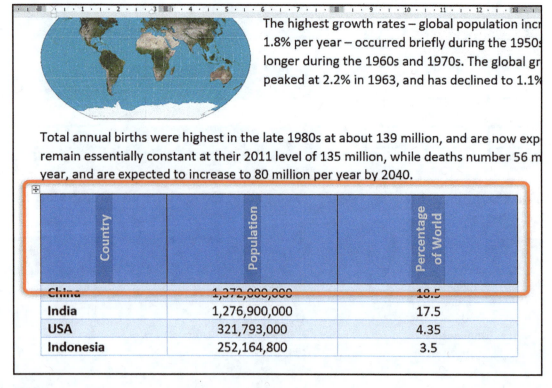

Each time you click 'text direction' the text will change orientation, so you may need to click a couple of times to get the one you want. For the example below, I had to click twice.

The highest growth rates – global population incr 1.8% per year – occurred briefly during the 1950s longer during the 1960s and 1970s. The global gr peaked at 2.2% in 1963, and has declined to 1.1%

Total annual births were highest in the late 1980s at about 139 million, and are now exp remain essentially constant at their 2011 level of 135 million, while deaths number 56 m year, and are expected to increase to 80 million per year by 2040.

Country	Population	Percentage of World
China	1,372,000,000	18.5
India	1,276,900,000	17.5
USA	321,793,000	4.35
Indonesia	252,164,800	3.5

Drawing a Table

When you need a table with a non-uniform structure, drawing allows you to create cells of varying sizes within the same row or column.

From the 'insert' ribbon tab, click on 'table'. From the dropdown menu, select 'draw table'.

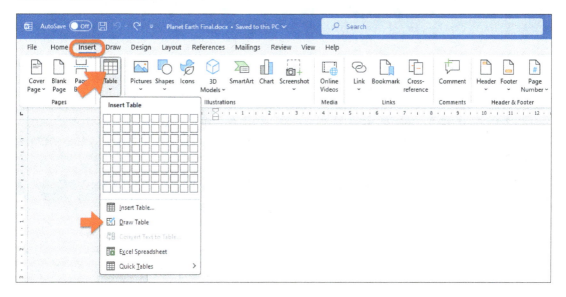

Click and drag your mouse to draw the outer boundaries of the table.

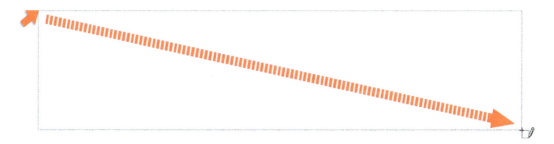

After drawing the outer boundary, you can draw the individual rows and columns by dragging the pencil cursor across the table. The table will be divided based on where you draw the lines.

Convert Text to Table

Converting text into a table is a useful feature when you have data separated by a consistent delimiter, such as commas or tabs. Here below my data is separated by a tab.

```
Country    Population       Percentage of World
China      1,372,000,000    18.5
India      1,276,900,000    17.5
USA        321,793,000      4.35
Indonesia  252,164,800      3.35
Brazil     204,878,000      2.77
```

To convert it to a table, highlight the text data in your Word document. From the insert ribbon tab, click on 'table'. From the drop down menu, select 'convert text to table'.

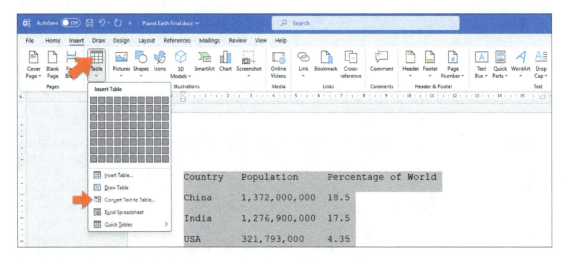

In the dialog box, you'll see an option for "separate text at". Choose "Tabs" since the data provided is separated by tabs.

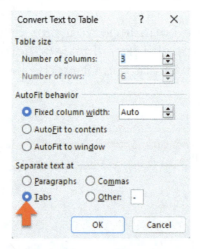

Adding a Chart

First, click the position in your document where you want your chart to appear. This will place your cursor in that position.

To insert a chart, click the insert ribbon, circled below. From the insert ribbon, click 'chart'.

From the insert chart dialog box, select the type of chart you want to insert.

Choosing the right chart type is important for effectively conveying your data. Each chart type has its unique purpose and visual representation. A pie chart is ideal for displaying parts of a whole, and showing data as percentages of the total. If you have distinct segments of data and want to 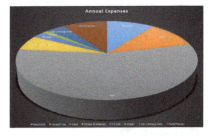 emphasize their proportion relative to the entire dataset, a pie chart is a suitable choice. For instance, it can vividly showcase the market share of various products within a company's sales.

A bar chart or a column chart is useful for comparing values across different categories or groups. If you need to visualize data grouped into categories (such as time periods, product names, or regions) and want to make comparisons across these categories, a bar chart is the one to use. For 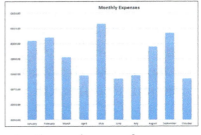 example, you might use a bar chart to illustrate the sales performance of different products over the course of a year.

A Line Chart is ideal for tracking trends and changes over time. It's the go-to choice when you wish to demonstrate how data points evolve in a continuous sequence or over regular intervals. A typical use case is displaying stock price fluctuations over a specific time period.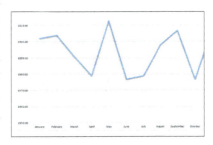

In this example, I am adding a pie chart to show my population statistics, so I'd click 'pie' then select a style from the selections.

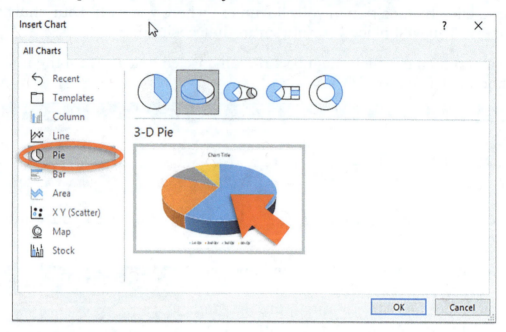

Click 'ok' when you're done.

Chart Data

Now that we have our blank chart, we need to add some data. In this example, I want to create a chart from the population table in the previous section.

You can copy and paste the data from the table into the chart DataSheet. To do this, click your cursor just before the 'C' in country and drag your mouse across the whole table so it's highlighted. Right click on the selection, and from the popup menu select 'copy'.

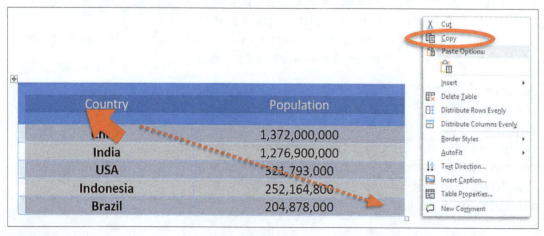

In the chart DataSheet, right click in the cell A1 and select paste.

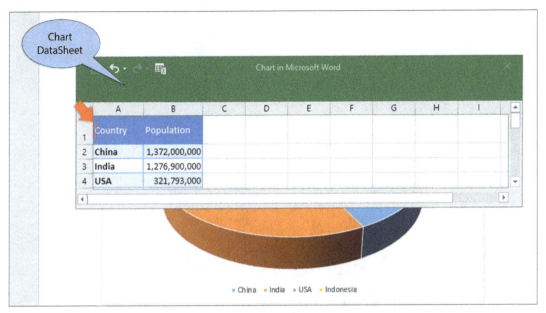

You can also type the data directly into the DataSheet.

Should you need to open up your DataSheet for your chart again, right click on your chart and select 'edit data'.

Chart Elements

To change any of the chart elements, first click on the chart to select it.

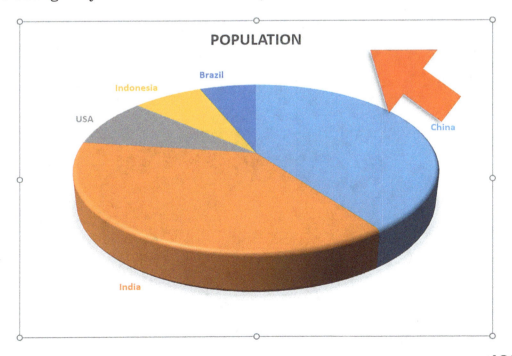

When you select your chart, you'll see four small icons appear on the top right of the chart.

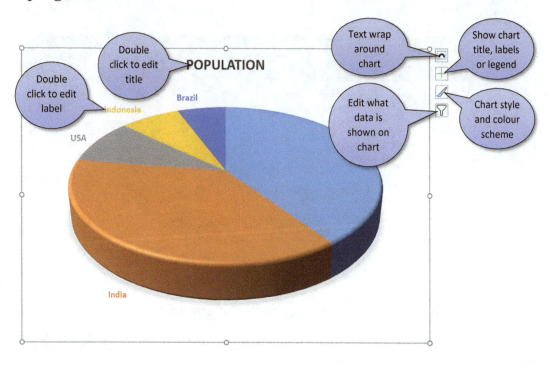

You can also edit the labels. To do this double click on the label then type in a name.

Chart Styles

To change the style of the chart or color scheme, first click on the chart to select it.

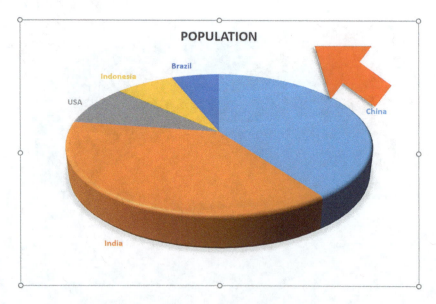

From the icons that appear, select the style icon circled below.

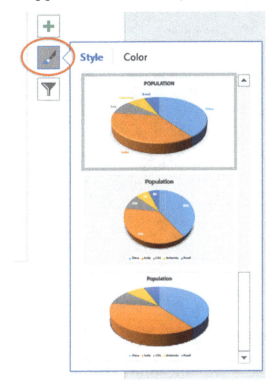

From the popup menu, select a pre-defined style. You can select a style with a legend or with each segment of the pie chart labelled. You could have your chart with rounded edges or sharp edges, with background shading or not, to name a few examples.

Data Filters

To only show certain data on your chart, you can use a filter. To do this, click on your chart to select it, then from the four icons on the top right, select the filter icon.

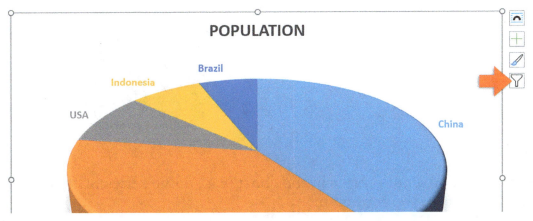

Now under the 'values' tab, select which data you want to show.

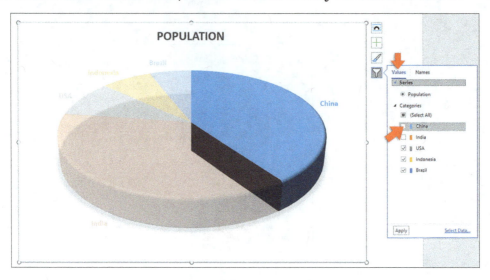

Click 'apply' at the bottom.

Advanced Charting Options

Microsoft Word offers advanced charting features that allow you to enhance the depth and clarity of your charts, making them more informative and visually appealing.

Trendlines

These are used to identify data trends and are used in line charts. Open your Word document with the chart you want to use. Click on the chart to select it.

Right-click on a data series in the chart (e.g., a line series). Choose 'add trendline' from the context menu.

In the 'format trendline' pane that appears on the right, you can customize the trendline type, style, and other options.

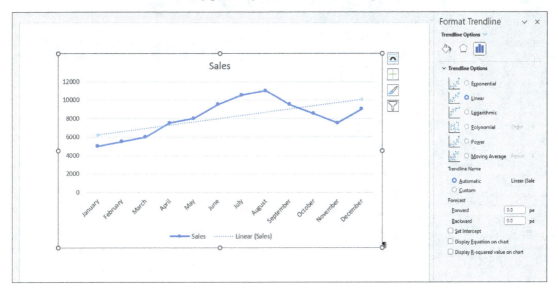

Secondary Axes

These facilitate the comparison of data with different scales, enhancing chart comprehensibility. If your line chart has only one data series, this option will be grayed out because there is no additional series to format.

Right click on the data series that you want to associate with a secondary axis. Choose 'format data series' from the menu.

In the side panel on the right hand side, go to the 'axis' section and check the box for "Secondary Axis."

6

Using Templates

Word templates are pre-designed documents that serve as starting points for creating new documents with a similar format, layout, and style. These templates can include various elements such as text, graphics, formatting, and placeholders for specific information. Microsoft Word provides a wide range of templates to simplify document creation for different purposes.

In this chapter, we'll explore how to use templates. We'll look at:

- Using Templates
- Finding a Template
- Making Your Own Template
- Create Document from Saved Template

To help you better understand this section, take a look at the video resources. Open your web browser and navigate to the following website:

elluminetpress.com/word-temp

You'll also need to download the source files from:

elluminetpress.com/word

Finding a Template

When you start Word, you will see a screen containing thumbnails of different templates that are available. To find templates, click 'new' on the left hand side.

The best way to find templates is to search for them.

As an example, I am going to build a CV/Resume. So, in the search field I'm going to type...

```
resume
```

In the search results, you'll see a whole range of different styles and designs. Double click on the template you want to use.

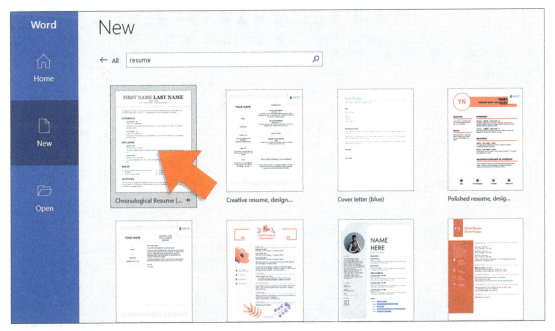

In the document that opens up, notice there are a number of fields. When you click on these fields they will be highlighted in grey. These are just place-holders where you can enter your information

FIRST NAME LAST NAME

Address · Phone
Email · LinkedIn Profile · Twitter/Blog/Portfolio

To replace this text with your own, just click it and start typing. Briefly state your career objective, or summarize what makes you stand out. Use language from the job description as keywords.

EXPERIENCE

DATES FROM – TO
JOB TITLE, COMPANY
Describe your responsibilities and achievements in terms of impact and results. Use examples, but keep it short.

DATES FROM – TO
JOB TITLE, COMPANY
Describe your responsibilities and achievements in terms of impact and results. Use examples,

Click on these and type in your information. You will also be able to fully edit the document as normal.

KEVIN **WILSON**

Technology Park, Liverpool, L33AF · 01234567890
office@elluminetpress.com · www.elluminetpress.com · #elluminetpress

Lorem ipsum dolor sit amet, consectetur adipiscing elit. Sed tortor ipsum, ullamcorper id viverra eget, luctus vel leo. Quisque at diam sit amet turpis egestas rhoncus ac nec justo. Praesent rutrum metus vitae mi consectetur convallis in vitae justo.

EXPERIENCE

2012 – 2018
DIRECTOR, ELLUMINET PRESS
Mauris luctus lacinia ante, vitae iaculis erat tempus vitae. Maecenas sodales facilisis nulla. Maecenas eu euismod dolor. Vestibulum interdum nibh semper, euismod tellus at, convallis enim.

DATES FROM – TO
JOB TITLE, COMPANY

There are lots of different templates to choose from. Try opening some templates for flyers and brochures.

Why not try making a greeting card for someone you know?

Open Word, click 'new' on the left hand side and type...

`greeting card`

...into the search field.

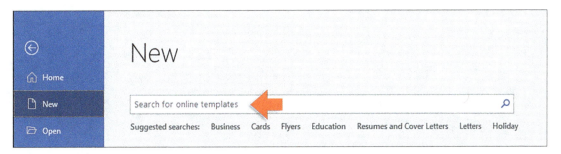

Select a template to use from the search results. How about a nice Christmas card?

Double click the template thumbnail, circled above, to open.

If you scroll down the page, you'll see some place holders where you can enter your own messages.

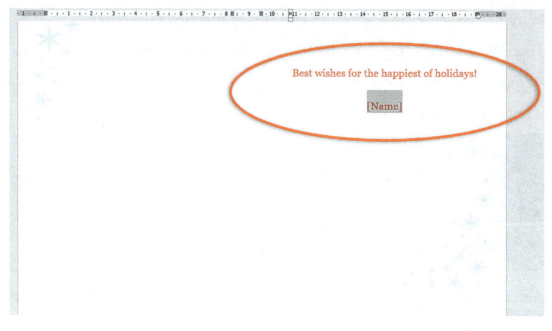

And here...

Just click on the text and enter your own.

Some of these templates need special paper and some need to be printed double sided to work. *You may need to change your printer settings to print on card or glossy paper. Check your printer instructions for specifics.*

Then just fold the printout along the lines, and you have a greeting card.

Making Your Own Template

If you have created your own style, eg heading sizes, fonts and layouts, you can save this as a template, so you can create new documents in the same style.

Before you save your document as a template, you may want to remove the content you have added, if any, and add some detail you want to appear on all your documents you create with this template, for example, the logo in the header.

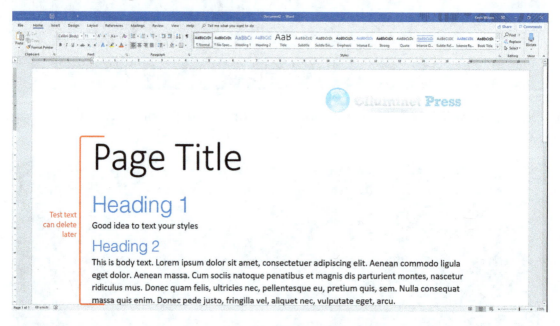

Also make sure your styles for headings and body text are as you want them. You can delete your test text before saving, leaving only what you want to appear in all documents as shown below.

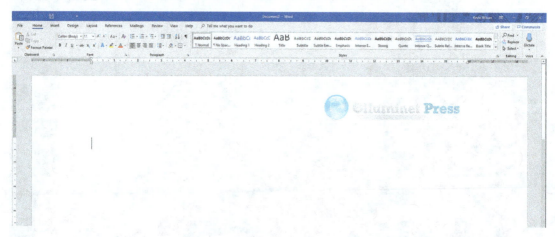

Now my template is ready to save.

To save your template, click 'file' and from the backstage click 'save as'. Click 'OneDrive' or 'This PC'. At the top of the 'save as' window, click 'more options'.

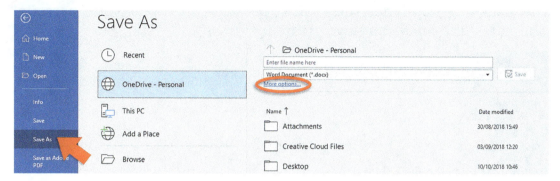

In the dialog box that appears, go down to 'save as type'. Click on the drop down box to open it up. From the drop down box, click 'Word Template (.dotx)'.

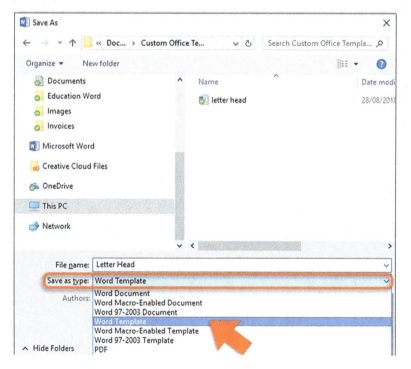

In the 'file name' field, give your template a name (eg letter head). Then click 'save'.

Note that the template is saved in

```
/Users/[your-user-name]/Library/Application Support/
Microsoft/Office/User Templates/My Templates
```

...not in your documents folders.

Create Document from Saved Template

To create a new document from your saved template, select 'new' from the backstage options, then click 'personal' to open your personal templates (the ones you have created yourself).

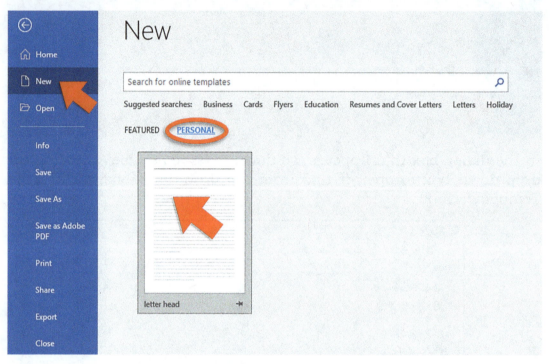

Double click the template thumbnail to open a new document.

Now we have a new document we can start editing.

You can add your text and content in the normal way.

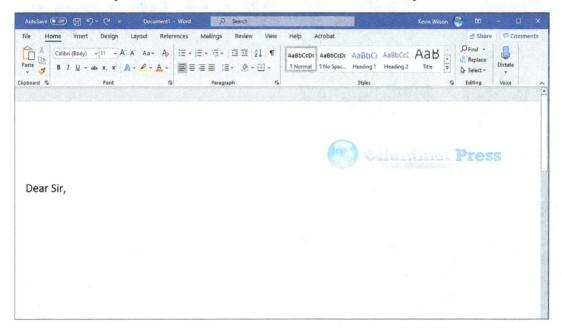

Once you're done, you can save the file. Select 'file' on the top left. Select 'save as'

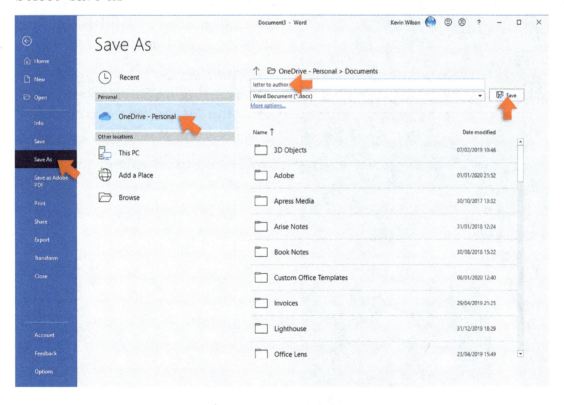

Select your 'onedrive', then select a folder to save your letter, eg 'documents'.

7

Mail Merge

Mail merge is a feature commonly used in Microsoft Word and similar applications, that allows you to create a batch of personalized documents, such as letters, envelopes, labels, or emails, from a single document and a data source such as a database or excel spreadsheet.

In this chapter, we'll explore how use mail merge to print labels and envelopes. We'll look at:

- Mail Merge
- Printing on Envelopes
- Mail Merge your Envelopes
- Mail Merge a Letter

You'll need to download the source files from:

elluminetpress.com/word

Printing on Envelopes

Word has templates for a large number of different size envelopes and has a feature that allows you to print your addresses in the correct position.

To start, click the mailings ribbon and select 'envelopes'

In the dialog box that appears, enter your recipient's address in 'delivery address'. If you want to include your return address, enter it in the 'return address' section, if not, click 'omit'.

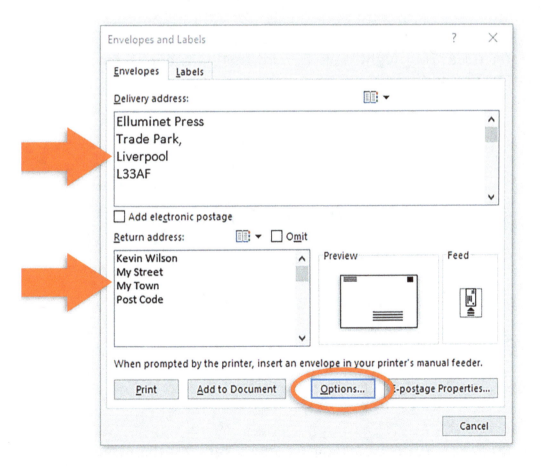

Next you'll need to select the size of your envelope. To do this, click 'options'.

From the dialog box that appears, select the size of the envelope from the drop down list. The sizes will be stated on the packet of envelopes you bought.

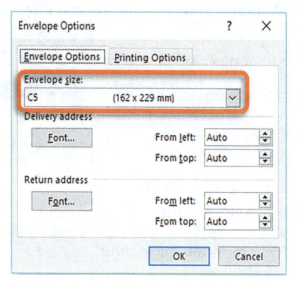

Next, click the 'printing options' tab and select the feed method your printer uses. You might have to read the instructions that came with your printer to find out.

My printer feeds the envelopes from the centre of the main paper tray, face up. So I'll select the 'centre feed method' and select 'face up' option.

Click OK when you're done.

Make sure you have loaded your envelope into your printer. Again, my printer feeds envelopes centred and face up, so this is how I have loaded the envelope into the tray. Note that this particular printer has paper guides that can be moved against the edge of the envelope to keep it in place. Check with your printer instructions for details on your specific printer.

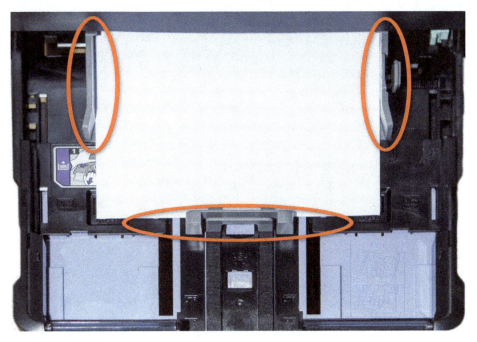

Now back at the main dialog box...

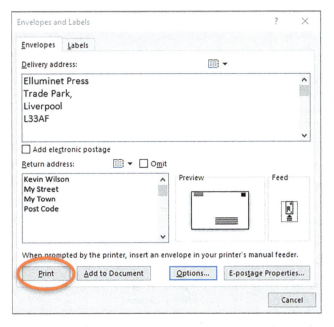

Click 'print' to print the envelope direct to your printer.

If you have a document or letter to go with the envelope, you can click 'add to document'. This will append the envelope to the top of your document.

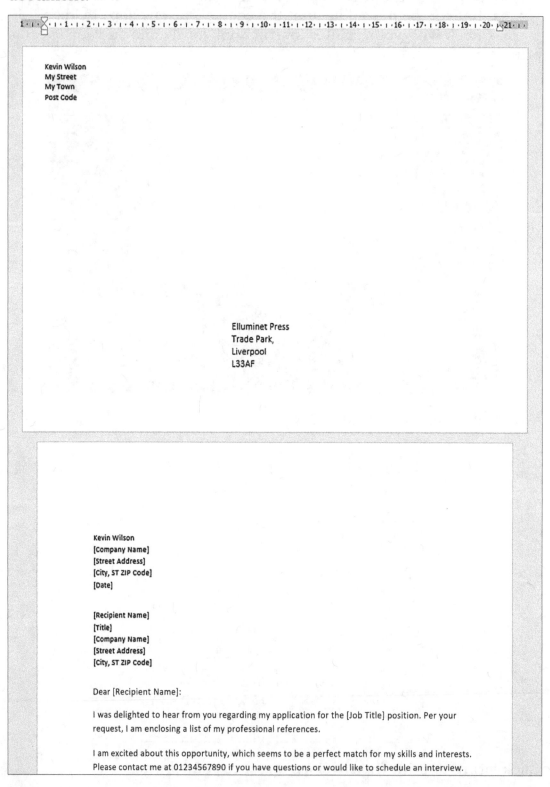

Mail Merge your Envelopes

If you have a lot of recipients, creating an envelope for each of them can be time consuming. This is where mail merge comes in handy.

First you'll need a data source. This is usually a list of names and addresses. A good place to keep names and addresses is in an excel spreadsheet. Also if you have added addresses to your Outlook 2019 contact list, you can import them from that.

I have a client list stored in an excel spreadsheet, so in this example, I will use that option. The procedure is the same if you use your Outlook contacts.

I have included some test data in a spreadsheet called Mail Merge Test Data.xlsx in the downloads section for you to practice with.

To select a data source, go to your mailings ribbon and click 'select recipients'.

From the drop down menu, click 'use an existing list...'.

In the dialog box that appears, find your data source. I'm going to select my excel spreadsheet. Mail Merge Test Data.xlsx

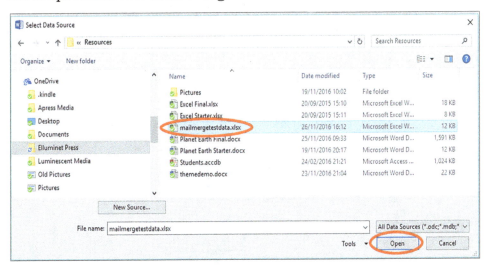

Click 'open'.

Chapter 7: Mail Merge

Now we can start the mail merge. You can mail merge letters, labels as well as envelopes. In this example I am going to merge envelopes.

From your mailings ribbon, click 'start mail merge' and select 'envelopes'.

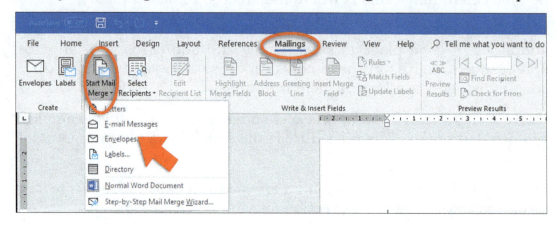

From the dialog box that appears, select the size of envelope from the 'envelope size' drop down list. The sizes are usually printed on the pack of envelopes you bought.

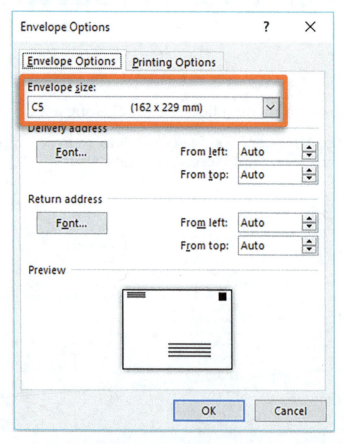

Next, click the 'printing options' tab.

Select the feed method your printer uses. You might have to read the instructions that came with your printer to find out.

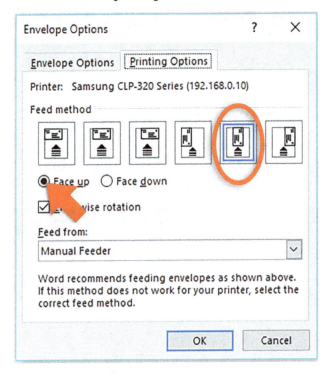

My printer feeds the envelopes from the centre of the main paper tray, face up. So I'll select the 'centre feed method' and select 'face up' option. Click OK when you're done.

Now to create your envelopes. First, find the address field in the template and click inside of it, as shown in the image below. Sometimes this is hidden but will appear once you click inside the field.

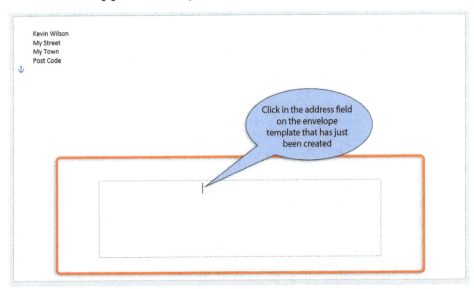

Next, from your mailings ribbon, click 'address block' to add the addresses from your contacts data source (Mail Merge Test Data.xlsx).

Click OK on the dialog box that pops up.

To preview your envelopes, from the mailings ribbon click 'preview results'. You can flip through the envelopes using the next/previous record icons.

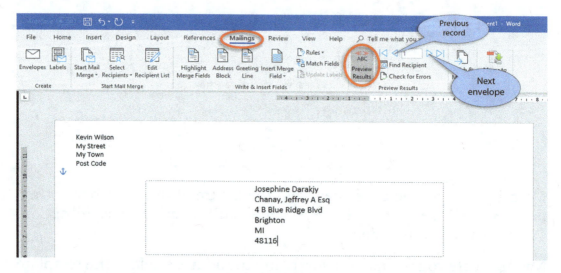

To finish off, from your mailings ribbon click 'finish & merge'. From the drop down menu, click 'print documents' to send the whole lot to the printer, make sure you have your envelopes already loaded into your printer's paper tray.

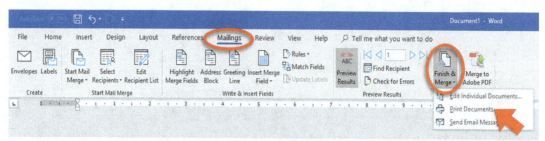

You can also click 'edit individual documents' and Word will generate a document with all your envelopes ready to print. This is useful if you want to make some changes or only print certain addresses.

Select 'all records' from the popup dialog box.

Mail Merge a Letter

Now that we have our envelopes printed, we need to write the letter. Mail merging a letter is a similar process.

First we need to write our letter. Open a blank document or use a letter template and write your letter. I have written an example below, leaving some space at the top for an address we'll add with mail merge.

Dear

We take great pleasure in welcoming your child to our school! I'm excited about the opportunity to get to know you, as well, and I'm looking forward to a happy and productive school year.

This year we will focus on the following curriculum areas:

- Maths
- English
- ICT
- Media
- Sciences
- Physical Education

If you have any questions or concerns, please contact me by email or phone. I also welcome appointments to meet in person. You can contact me on 0151 1234567 or kevin.wilson@anewschool.sch.uk.

Let's work together to make this the best year ever!

Sincerely,

Kevin Wilson
Headmaster

Now that we have our letter, we need to add some fields to address these letters to each recipient.

We need to insert their address on the top right, and their name in the first line of the letter. These names and addresses can be stored in a spreadsheet or database. Just like we did when we mail merged our envelopes, we need to select a data source.

I have included some test data in a spreadsheet called Mail Merge Test Data.xlsx in the downloads section for you to practice with.

To connect your data source, select your mailings ribbon and click 'select recipients'. From the drop down menu, select 'use an existing list'.

Then select your data file. For this example, I'm using Mail Merge Test Data.xlsx.

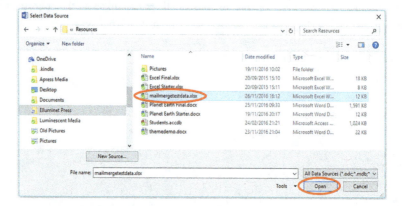

Click 'open' on the dialog box. Now we can start adding our names and addresses to the letter. Click to position your cursor where the address lines will be, eg first name followed by last name will appear top left, so click on the top left of your document to position your cursor.

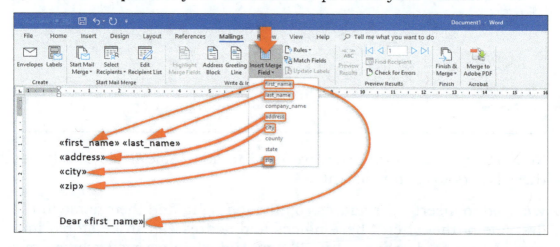

From the mailings ribbon, click 'insert merge field', then from the drop down select 'first_name', press space bar on your keyboard, then click 'insert merge field' and select 'last_name'. Press return and repeat the process to add the rest of the address.

Once you have added all the fields, from the mailings ribbon click 'preview results'. You'll get something like this (a letter for each name and address):

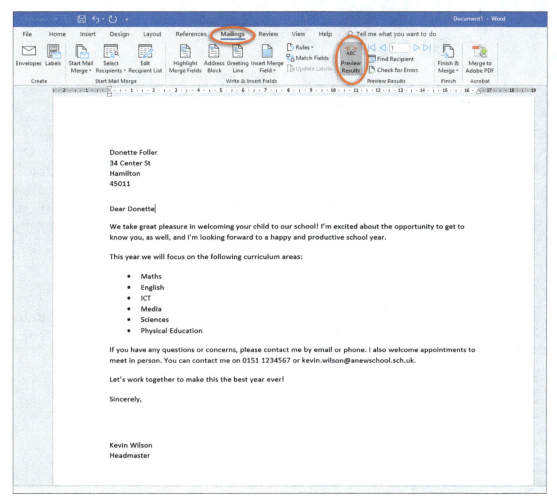

To finish off, from the mailings ribbon, click 'finish & merge'

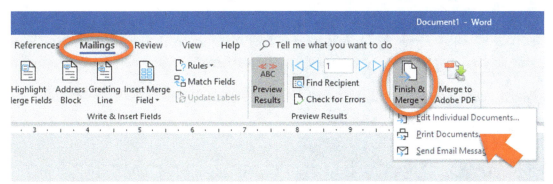

To send all letters to the printer click, 'print documents'. To open all merged letters in a document click 'edit individual documents'.

8

Proofing and Markup

Proofing and Markup tools are designed to enhance the document writing and editing process. Whether you're a writer, editor, student, or professional, these features provide support for reviewing, checking and improving your text.

In this chapter, we'll explore how to use the spelling and grammar checks, and how to improve your writing. We'll look at:

- Proofing and Markup
- Check your Spelling & Grammar
- Editing your Custom Dictionary
- Thesaurus
- Researcher
- AutoText
- AutoCorrect

You'll need to download the source files from:

elluminetpress.com/word

Spelling & Grammar

To check your document, click the review ribbon then select 'editor'.

You'll notice on the right hand side of your screen, Word has found a spelling issue, no grammar issues and one refinement. Refinements are intended to make your document clearer and easier to read.

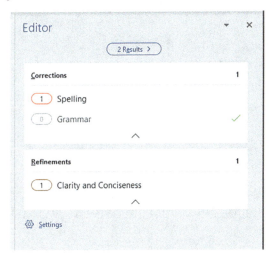

To review these corrections, click on them in the list. First click 'spelling', you'll see the errors highlighted in your document.

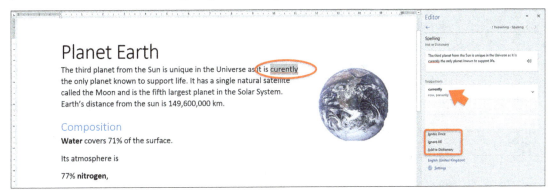

Click on the suggested correction shown in the panel on the right hand side. If the word is a proper noun such as a place name or person's name and the spelling is correct, you can either click 'ignore all' to ignore all uses of the word, or click 'add to dictionary' to add the word to your custom dictionary.

Chapter 8: Proofing and Markup

Continuing with the spell & grammar check, Word has found some refinements to make our document clearer. Now this feature isn't 100% accurate but can give some good examples of how to word sentences more clearly. On the editor panel on the right hand side, click 'clarity and conciseness'

You'll see Word has found a better way to write the sentence. Instead of saying "a number of..." we could use the word "several", as shown below.

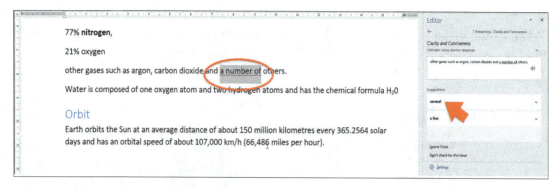

Other gases such as argon, carbon dioxide and <u>a number of</u> others

Can be changed to

Other gases such as argon, carbon dioxide and <u>several</u> others

So, select 'several' from the suggestions on the right hand side of your screen.

Real-time Spell & Grammar Check

You can also check spelling and grammar within the document as you type. Spelling errors are underlined in red, grammar errors are underlined in blue. Possible errors or improvements are usually indicated in dark red dotted line. Notice, there are some errors below.

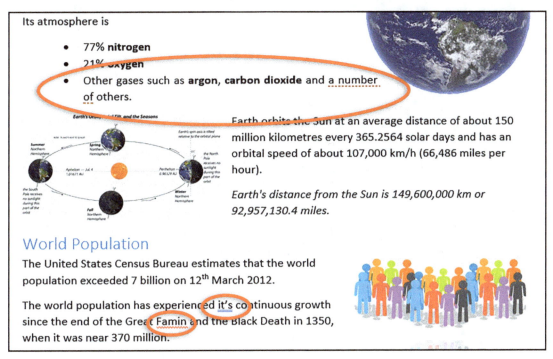

You can quickly correct these. To do this, right click your mouse on the word.

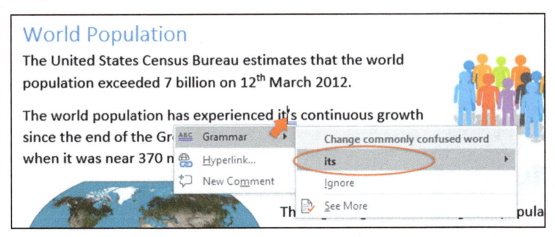

From the popup menu that appears, you'll see Word's suggestion. In this example, the word 'it's' is used instead of 'its' - word used in wrong context. Click the correct word in the suggestions and Word will make the correction.

You can do the same for spelling errors. Right click the error and select the correct word from the suggestions.

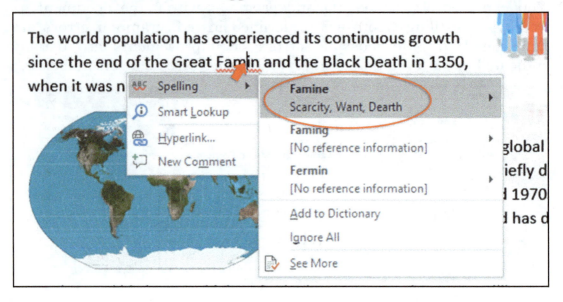

Editing your Custom Dictionary

To edit a custom dictionary, click 'file', then select 'options' from the list on the left hand side.

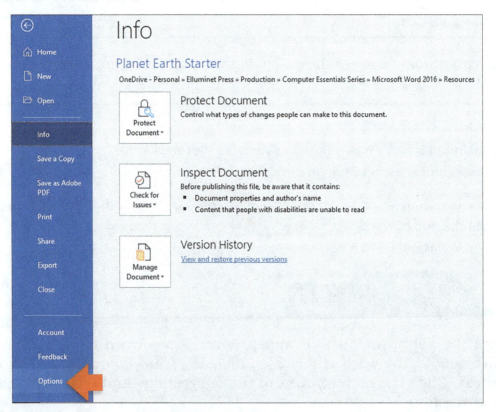

From the dialog box that appears, select 'proofing', then select 'custom dictionaries'.

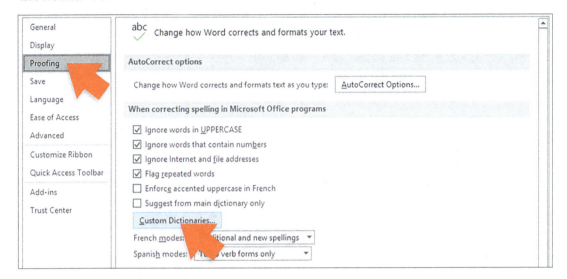

Select your custom dictionary. This is usually called 'custom.dic' or similar.

From here, you can delete words - just click the word you want to remove and click 'delete'.

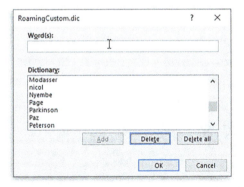

Similarly, to add a word, type the word into the field at the top of the dialog box and click 'add'. Click 'ok' when you're done.

Thesaurus

In our text, if I wanted to find a synonym for the word 'exceeded', I can do that quite easily. To find a synonym, right click on the word you want, then from the popup menu, go down to 'synonyms'.

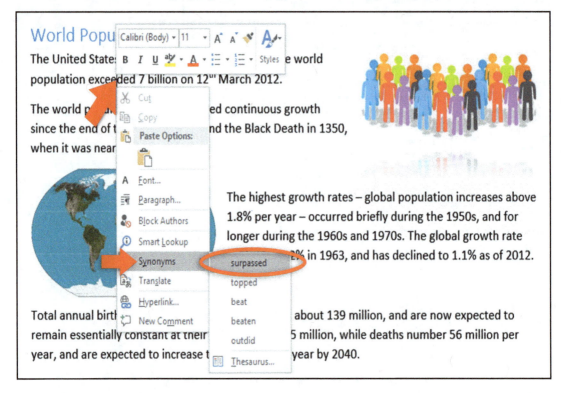

A slide out menu will appear with some suggested synonyms. Click the most appropriate one for your word. Word will substitute the selected synonym.

Researcher

With researcher you can view information from online sources within Word itself. Word can gather information from online encyclopedias, web searches and other online sources. To do this, select the 'references' ribbon tab. In the 'research' section, you'll see two options. Click on researcher.

The researcher bar will open on the right hand side of your screen. Here you'll see a search field where you can type in your research topics. Scroll through and click on the topics to view. To add a citation for the source to your bibliography, click the small plus icon on the right hand side of the topic. You'll see the citation appear at your cursor, as well as a bibliography page.

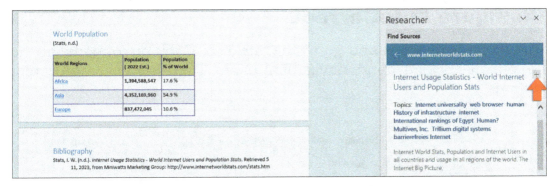

To look something up, click on a particular key word, or highlight a name or heading and click 'search'. *You can also click on the 'references' ribbon tab, then select 'search'.* The search panel will open on the right hand side. Select 'files' to search in your Word documents, 'this file' to search your open Word document, or click 'media' to search for images.

In this example, I have selected 'images', as I want a picture of Earth for my report. Click and drag the images to your document if you choose to use them.

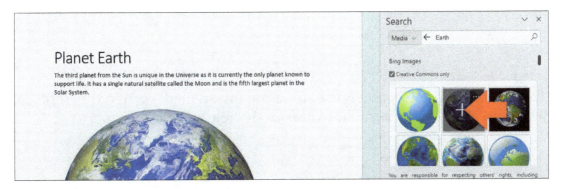

AutoCorrect and AutoText

AutoCorrect and AutoText are two helpful features in Microsoft Word that can save you time and improve your productivity when working on documents.

Configure AutoCorrect

Open Microsoft Word and go to the 'file' tab. Click on 'options' at the bottom of the left-hand navigation pane. Then select 'AutoCorrect Options'.

This opens the AutoCorrect dialog box. Here you'll find a list of common replacements. This list is quite extensive so before adding any new replacements, check to see if it's already added.

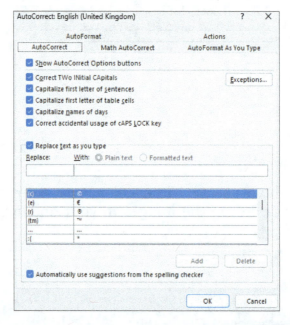

To add a new AutoCorrect entry, type the misspelled word in the 'replace' field and the correct version in the 'with' field. Click 'add'.

As you type, Word will automatically correct common misspellings based on the entries you've configured in AutoCorrect. For example, if you type "teh," Word will automatically replace it with "the."

AutoText

AutoText is a feature that allows you to store and quickly insert frequently used pieces of text or content into your documents. These text snippets can range from a single word or phrase to entire paragraphs or pages.

First, highlight the text or content that you want to save as an AutoText entry. Go to the 'insert' ribbon tab.

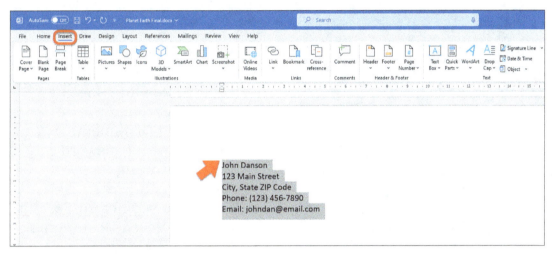

Select 'AutoText' from the dropdown menu, and then choose 'Save Selection to AutoText Gallery'. Give the AutoText entry a name.

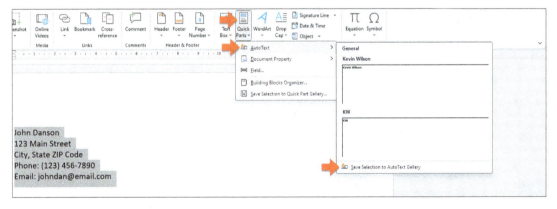

To use the entry, place your cursor where you want to insert the AutoText. Go to the 'insert' ribbon tab, select 'quick parts', then go down to 'AutoText'.

Select the 'AutoText' entry you want to add to your document.

9

Managing Documents

In this chapter, we'll explore how to manage your documents. We'll look at:

- Reading Documents Aloud
- Reading Documents
- Change Reading Speed
- Changing Voices
- Protecting Documents
- Encrypt with Password
- Restrict Editing
- Saving Documents
- Saving as a Different Format
- Opening Saved Documents
- Printing Documents
- Page Setup
- Simple Macros

To help you better understand this section, take a look at the video resources. Open your web browser and navigate to the following website:

elluminetpress.com/word-man

You'll also need to download the source files from:

elluminetpress.com/word

Reading Documents Aloud

The read aloud feature reads your document out loud using a synthesized voice.

Reading Documents

To run this feature, open the document you want to read, then from the 'review' ribbon tab, click 'read aloud'. Make sure your audio is on and volume is turned up.

As Word reads the document, you'll see a marker move across your text. On the top right of the document you'll see some controls.

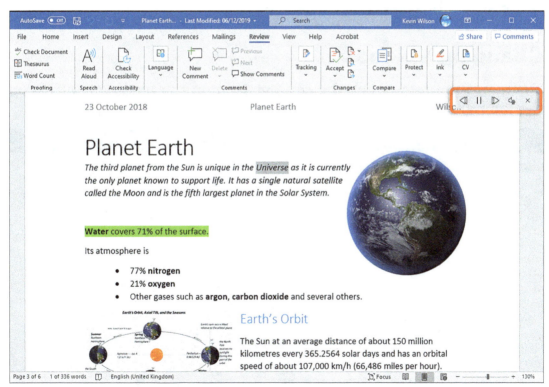

Here, you can jump back to the start of a paragraph, start or stop the reading, jump forward, and adjust settings.

Change Reading Speed

To change the reading speed, click the settings icon on the reading controls on the top right of the screen.

Use the slider to adjust the speed.

Slide the slider to the right to speed up reading, slide the slider to the left to slow it down.

Changing Voices

To change the voice, click the settings icon on the reading controls on the top right of the screen.

From the 'voice selection' drop down box you can select between three voices.

Protecting Documents

You can lock a document to prevent anyone opening or editing it without a password. To do this, click 'file' on the top left.

Select 'info', then click the 'protect document button'.

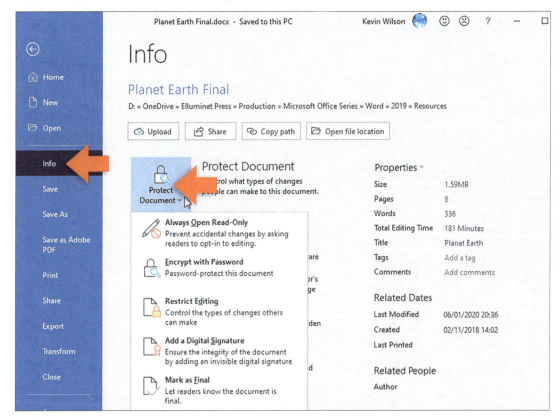

Always open read only allows you to lock a document to prevent changes. User's can easily turn this off when they open the document so this option isn't secure.

Encrypt with password allows you to lock the document so you can only open and edit it with a password.

Restrict editing allows you to give people permission to read and edit parts of your document.

Add a digital signature allows you to sign important documents electronically to validate your identity and ensure the documents are legitimate.

Mark as final makes your documents read only. This means typing, editing, and proofing marks are disabled, and the status property of the document is set to 'final'.

Encrypt with Password

To encrypt a document with a password, click 'file' on the top left. Select 'info', then click the 'protect document button'.

Select 'encrypt with password' from the drop down menu.

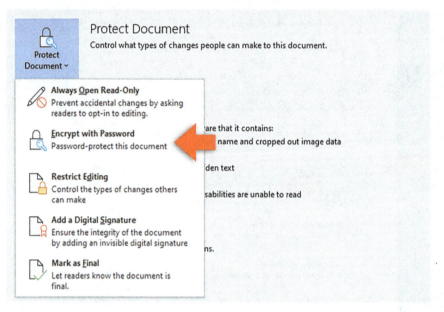

Enter a password into the popup dialog box.

Save the document.

Anyone who tries to open the document will be prompted for the password.

To remove the encryption, open the document and enter the password. Go to File > Info > Protect Document. Click 'encrypt with password'. Clear the password in the password box, then click 'ok'.

Restrict Editing

To restrict editing, click 'file' on the top left. Select 'info', then click the 'protect document button'.

Select 'restrict editing' from the drop down menu.

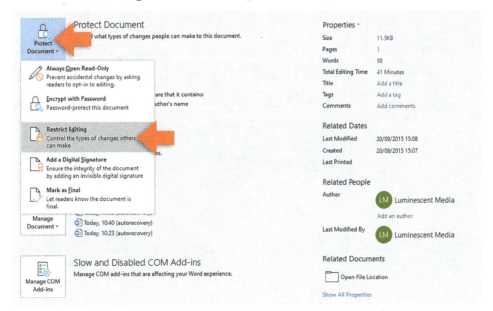

Select the part of the document you want to allow edits.

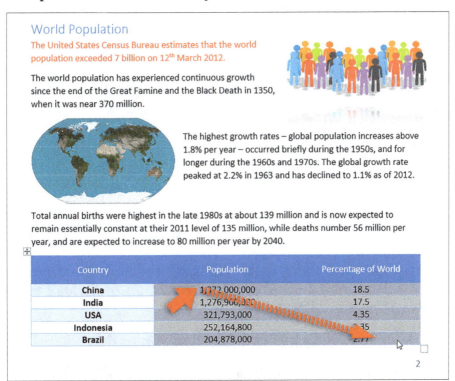

Chapter 9: Managing Documents

From the panel on the right hand side select 'allow this type of editing in this document'. Then select the users to allow access or select 'everyone' for all users who open the document.

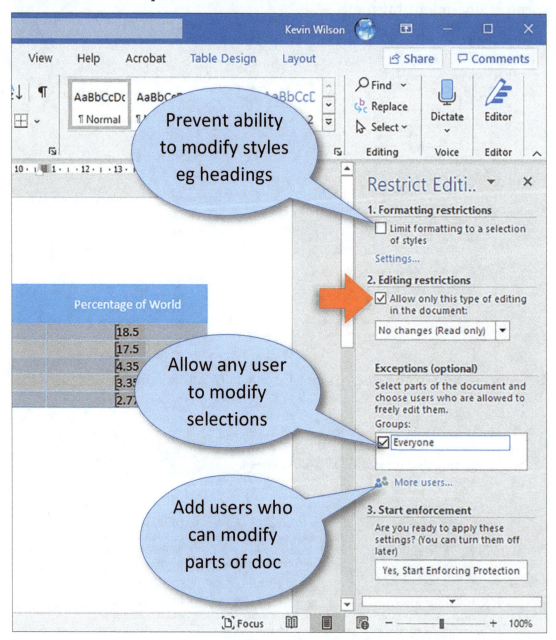

If you want to prevent users from changing the styles such as heading font or size select 'limit formatting to a selection of styles', then select the styles you want to allow.

Click 'yes, start enforcing protection' when you're done.

Enter a password. You'll need this to remove the protection.

Saving Documents

To save your work, click the small disk icon in the top left hand corner of the screen.

In the save as screen, you need to tell Word where you want to save the document.

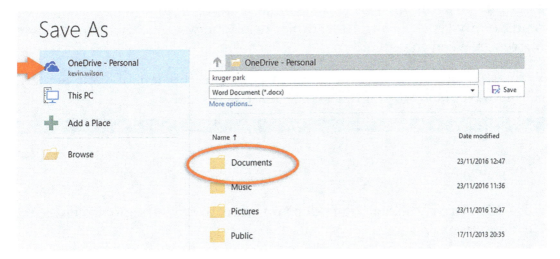

Save it onto "OneDrive Personal", in the documents/word folder created in the previous section. Click OneDrive, Double click 'documents', then double click 'Word'.

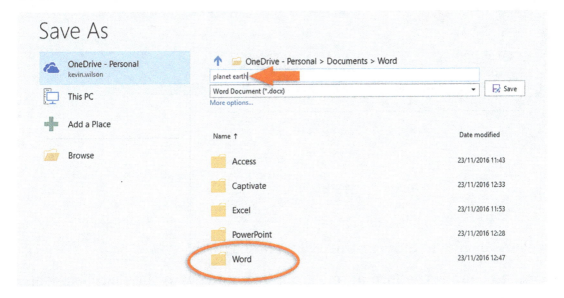

In text box, indicated above with the red arrow, type in a meaningful name describing the work. In this case "planet earth"

Click Save. This will save directly to your OneDrive account.

Saving as a Different Format

Sometimes you'll want to save a document in a different format. This can be useful if you are sending a document to someone that might not be using Windows or have Microsoft Office installed.

Word allows you to save your document in different formats. A common example is saving files as PDFs, which is a portable format that can be read on any type of computer, tablet or phone without the need to have Microsoft Word installed.

With your document open, click File on the top left of your screen. Select 'save as' from the list on the left hand side.

Click 'OneDrive', select the folder you want to save the document into. Eg 'documents'.

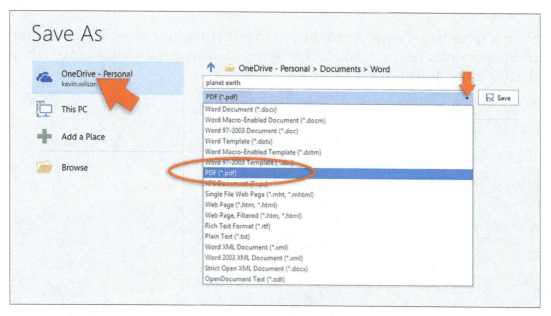

Give your file a name, in this case 'planet earth'

Now to change the format, click the down arrow in the field below and from the list, click PDF

You can also save as a web page, rich text and so on. Bear in mind that you may lose certain formatting and effects if they are not supported in these formats.

Opening Saved Documents

If Word is already open you can open previously saved documents by clicking the FILE menu on the top left of your screen.

From the blue bar along the left hand side click 'open'.

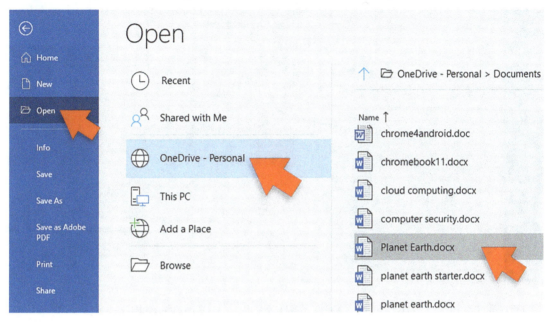

From the list, select the document you want to open. The document from the previous project was saved as 'planet earth.docx', so this is the one I am going to open here.

For convenience, Microsoft Word lists all your most recently opened documents. To do this click 'recent'. On the right hand side, click 'documents' to view recently opened documents, click 'folders' to see recently accessed folders.

Your latest files will be listed first. Double click the file name to open it.

Printing Documents

To print a document, click FILE on the top left of your screen.

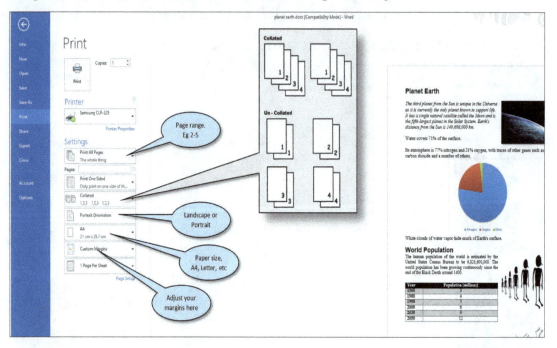

Down the left hand side, you can select options such as number of copies, print individual pages instead of the whole document and adjust layout and margins.

You can adjust margins, and print pages in either landscape or portrait orientation. Portrait tends to be more for documents or letters, while landscape works well with pictures and photos.

Once you have set all your options, click the print button at the top.

Page Setup

Page setup allows you to adjust margins, paper size, orientation (landscape/portrait) and general layout.

To adjust your page setup, go to your layout tab and click the expand icon on the bottom right of the page setup section.

From the dialog box that appears, you'll see your margin, paper and layout tabs.

You can adjust the margins as shown below. The top and bottom margins are color coded in blue and the left and right margins are color coded in red.

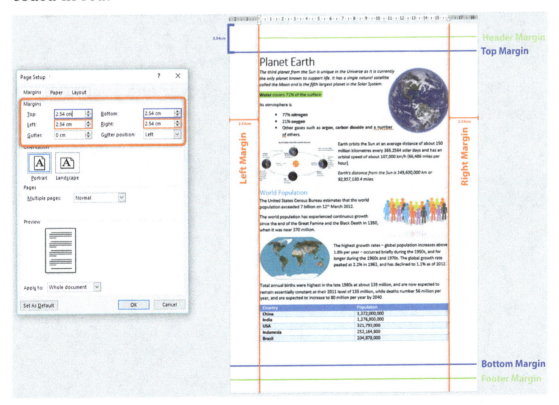

If you look in the margins tab, you'll see these sizes measured in centimetres (or inches). This is the distance from the physical edge of the page. The relevant fields in the margins tab are color coded accordingly so you can see how it works.

If we move to the next tab 'Paper', we can change the paper size (legal, A4 or A3).

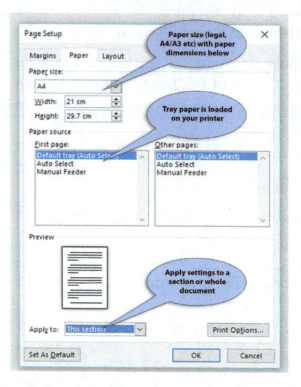

The last tab 'layout', allows you to change the header and footer margins.

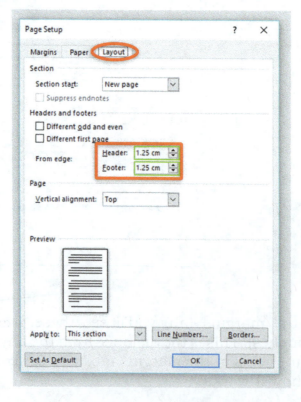

This is the distance the header appears from the physical edge of the page.

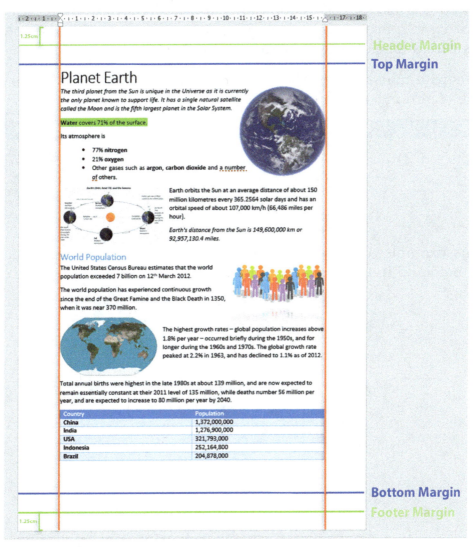

In the layout tab, you can set 'different odd and even' headers. When you enable this option, Word will automatically create two separate header and footer sections in your document. The odd-page section will be applied to all odd-numbered pages, and the even-page section will be applied to all even-numbered pages. This is useful if you want to include different content on the left and right pages of a book or if you want to include page numbers on the outside edge of each page.

When you enable 'different first page', Word creates a separate header or footer for the first page of the document or section, and then applies a different header or footer to all subsequent pages. This means that you can have different content, such as a title or logo, on the first page of your document, without that content appearing on subsequent pages.

Recording Macros

A macro is a is a set of actions and instructions that you can record or written in a programming language to perform repetitive or complex tasks with a single click or keyboard shortcut.

To record a macro, go to the 'view' ribbon tab, click on 'macros' then select 'record macro' from the menu.

In this example, we'll record a macro that applies specific formatting (e.g., bold and italic) to selected text.

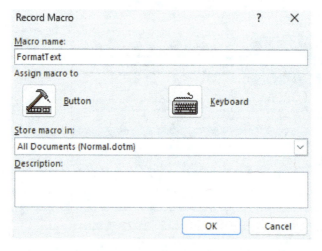

In the 'Record Macro' dialog box, enter a name for your macro, for example "FormatText".

Click 'button' to add the macro to a command button to the quick access toolbar. Click on the macro in the left column, then select 'add.

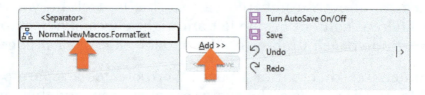

Choose where to store the macro ("This Document" or "New Document").

Click 'ok' to start recording.

Perform the actions you want to record. For example

1. Select a portion of text in your document.

2. Click on the "Bold" and "Italic" buttons on the home ribbon to apply these formatting options to the selected text.

When you're done, go back to the view ribbon tab, click on 'macros', then select 'Stop Recording' to finish recording the macro.

You'll see the new macro appear on the quick access toolbar on the top left of the screen. Now, to use the macro, select some text, then click the icon on the quick access toolbar.

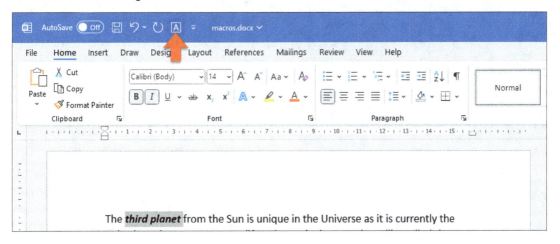

To view all your macros, go to the 'view' ribbon, click 'macros' then select 'view macros'.

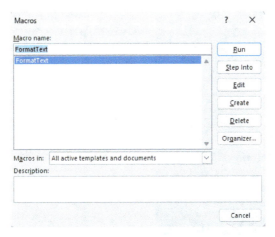

10

Sharing & Collaboration

Sharing involves actively providing other users access to a document, enabling them to view or edit, based on defined permissions.

Collaboration is a collective, interactive effort where multiple individuals work together on a shared document by contributing ideas, feedback, and making edits in real-time.

To share and collaborate on documents you'll need a Microsoft account. Anyone you share the document with will also need a Microsoft account. Also, documents need to be saved on OneDrive or SharePoint to enable real-time collaboration.

The person sharing the document can set specific permissions, determining whether recipients can edit, comment on, or only view the document.

You'll need to download the source files from:

elluminetpress.com/word

Introduction

Microsoft Office applications such as Word, Excel, and PowerPoint allow You to save your files directly to OneDrive, making it easy to access files across all your devices.

On your PC/Mac, OneDrive creates a special folder that is synchronized with your OneDrive cloud storage. Any files or folders that you save to the OneDrive folder on your PC will automatically be uploaded to the cloud, and any changes made to files in the cloud will be copied back to the OneDrive folder on your PC. This is called synchronisation.

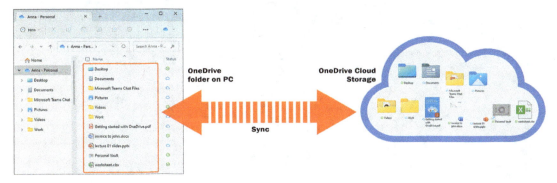

On mobile devices you can access all your OneDrive files without having to download them all to your device. This is called 'Files On-Demand'. This means all of your files and folders on OneDrive will be visible, but they are not be downloaded to your device until you actually need them. This feature saves space on your device and allows you to access your files from anywhere, even if you don't have enough storage on your local device.

OneDrive comes pre-installed on Windows 10/11 and you can access it through the File Explorer.

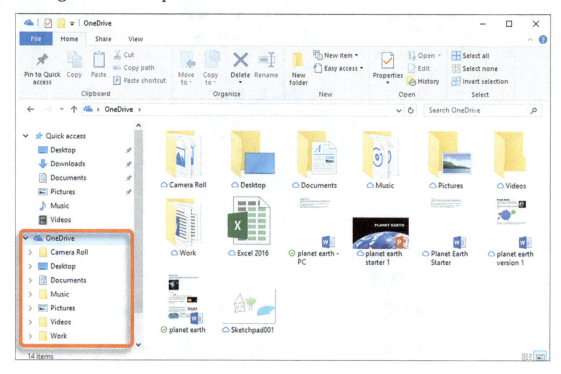

On a Mac, you can download the OneDrive app from the App Store. You'll find a OneDrive folder in the Finder app, and a shortcut to the OneDrive app along the top of the menu bar.

You can install the OneDrive app on mobile devices such as iPhones, iPads, and Android devices using the App Store.

You can access OneDrive on the web using a web browser such as Chrome, Safari or Edge.

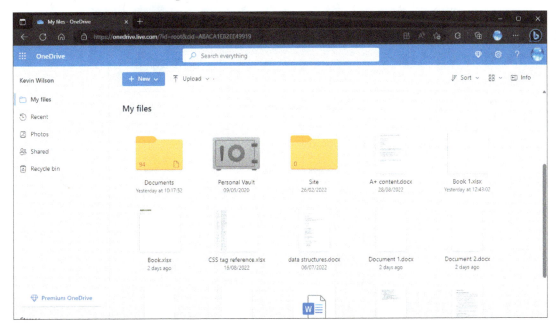

Collaborating in Word

Collaborating in Microsoft Word is a straightforward process. You can collaborate with others through the usual office apps such as Word, Excel and PowerPoint as well as Microsoft Teams, SharePoint, and OneDrive. For example, you can share a Word document with someone else using OneDrive.

Sharing a Document

To do this, click 'share' on the top right of your screen. You can do this in Word, Excel and PowerPoint. From the drop down menu select 'share'.

In this example, I'm going to share the document with someone else. To do this, type in the person's email address, then type in a message below if applicable.

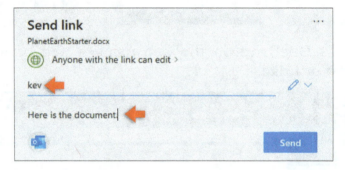

On the right hand side of the window, you'll see some sharing options. Select whether people will be able to edit the document or just view. In this example, I'm going to allow edits. Click send.

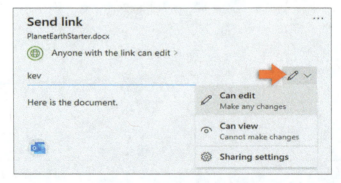

When your friend/colleague checks their email, they will be invited to open the document. Click 'view in OneDrive' to open.

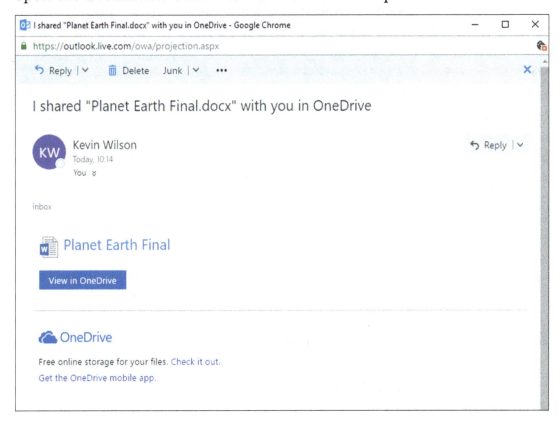

They will also see the document listed in the 'shared with me' section on the home screen when you start the Word desktop app.

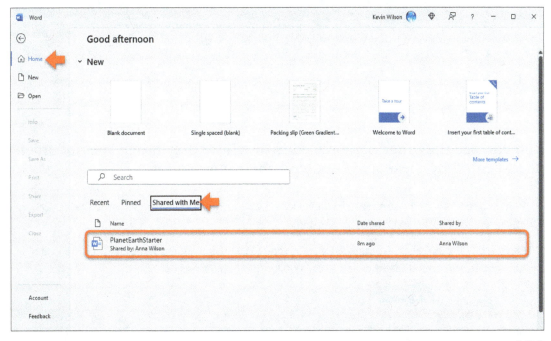

From here, your colleague/friend can edit or view the document. If they have Word installed on their machine, they can download and work on the document in Word. If they don't, they can work on the document online, within their web browser.

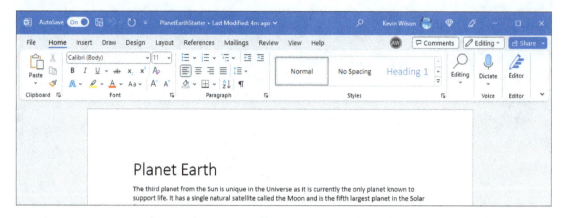

This is useful if you are working on a project with more than one person. Each person you shared the document with can edit and add content.

Real-Time Co-Authoring

Once you've opened a shared document, you'll see the other person's avatar appear in the menu bar on the top right of the screen. Here, you can jump to the location in the document this person is working on, or you can send them an email message.

You can see the other person's edits or where they are in the document as indicated by these markers with their name on it.

Water covers 71% of the surface. Its atmosphere is 77% nitrogen, 21% oxygen, other gases such as argon, carbon dioxide and a number of others.

Earth orbits the Sun at an average distance of about 150 million kilometres every 365.2564 solar days and has an orbital speed of about 107,000 km/h (66,486 miles per hour).

World Population | Anna Wilson

Commenting

You can add comments to parts of the document. To do this, first select & highlight the word, paragraph or image you want to comment on. Click 'comments' on the top right of the screen. In the comment dialog box, type in your comment, then click the post icon.

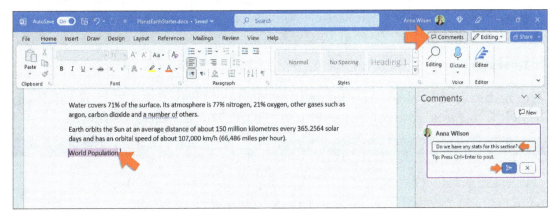

Your comment will appear in the comments sidebar linked to the highlighted text that was commented on.

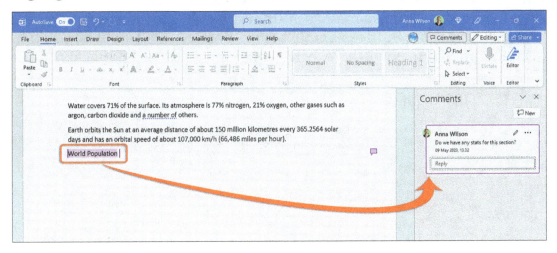

If you want to reply to the comment, type a message into the 'reply' field under the comment.

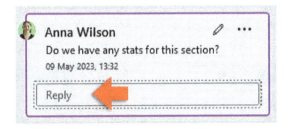

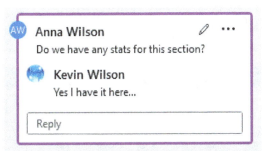

Track Changes

The "Track Changes" feature is primarily used for reviewing and editing documents collaboratively. It allows multiple users to make edits, comments, and suggestions to a document while keeping a record of all changes. This feature is particularly useful for authors, editors, and anyone who needs to track the progress of a document's revisions.

Enable

To enable track changes, go to the 'review' ribbon tab, then click on 'Track Changes'. Select 'for everyone' from the drop down menu.

Once activated, this feature will begin recording all changes made to the document. Any changes made are underlined in red. Any deletions are crossed out in red. In the example below, I've added a 'world population section' and changed 'fifth' to '5th'. You can see these changes in red.

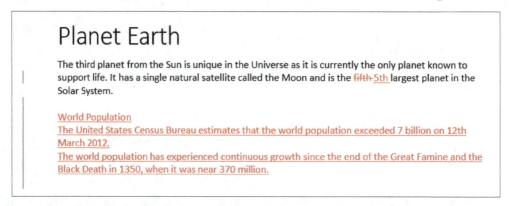

When you're making a lot of edits, sometimes the document can get very confusing. There are two options for displaying markup: "Simple Markup" and "All Markup." You can change this using the 'markup' drop down menu in the 'review' ribbon tab.

If you choose "Simple Markup" in dropdown menu, Word displays a simplified view of the document with minimal distractions. Simple Markup displays a vertical line in the margin next to any text that has been edited or commented on. If you choose "All Markup", Word displays all tracked changes, comments, and markup in the document.

Accepting and Rejecting Changes

After edits have been made, you can review each change individually and decide whether to accept or reject it. To do this, navigate through the document using the 'previous' and 'next' buttons on the 'review' tab.

Click 'accept' to keep the change, or 'reject' to discard it. You can also choose to accept or reject all changes in the document at once.

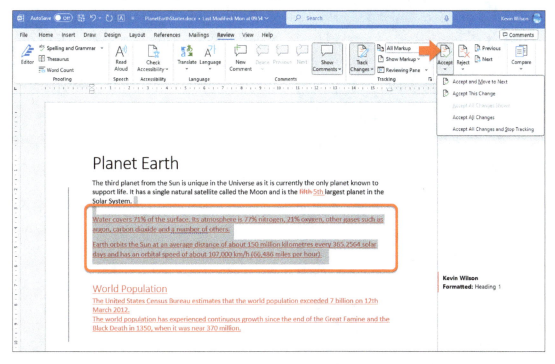

Once all edits and revisions are reviewed and accepted, you can choose to accept all changes and turn off Track Changes, resulting in a clean, final document. Click 'accept all changes and stop tracking'.

Resources

To help you understand the procedures and concepts explored in this book, we have developed some video resources and app demos for you to use, as you work through the book.

To find the resources, open your web browser and navigate to the following website

elluminetpress.com/ms-word

At the beginning of each chapter, you'll find a website that contains the resources for that chapter.

File Resources

To save the files into your OneDrive documents folder, right click on the icons above and select 'save target as' (or 'save link as', on some browsers). In the dialog box that appears, select 'OneDrive', click the 'Documents' folder, then click 'save'.

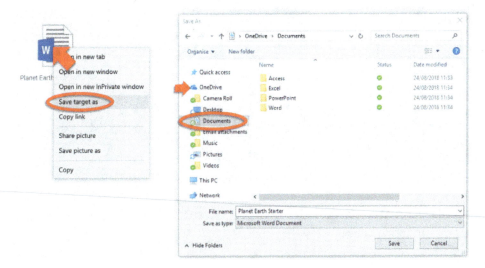

The sample images are stored in a compressed zip file. To download the zip file, right click on the zip icon on the page above, 'Sample Images. zip. Select 'save target as' (or 'save link as', on some browsers) and save it into 'pictures' on your OneDrive folder.

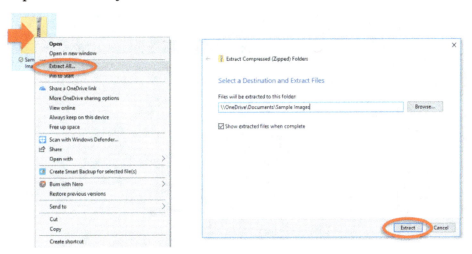

Once you have downloaded the zip file, go to your 'pictures' folder in your OneDrive, right click on the zip file, and select 'extract all' from the menu. From the dialog box that appears click 'extract'. This will create a new folder in your pictures called 'sample images'. You'll find the images used in the examples in the books.

Video Resources

The video resources are grouped into sections for each chapter in the book. Click the thumbnail link to open the section.

When you open the link to the video resources, you'll see a thumbnail list at the bottom.

Click on the thumbnail for the particular video you want to watch. Most videos are between 30 and 60 seconds outlining the procedure, others are a bit longer.

When the video is playing, hover your mouse over the video and you'll see some controls...

Let's take a look at the video controls. On the left hand side:

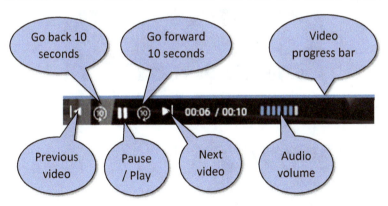

On the right hand side:

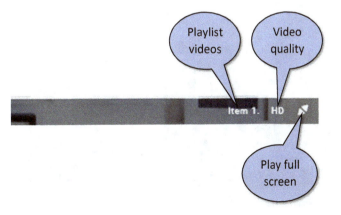

Scanning the Codes

At the beginning of each chapter, you'll a QR code you can scan with your phone to access additional resources, files and videos.

iPhone

To scan the code with your iPhone/iPad, open the camera app.

Frame the code in the middle of the screen. Tap on the website popup at the top.

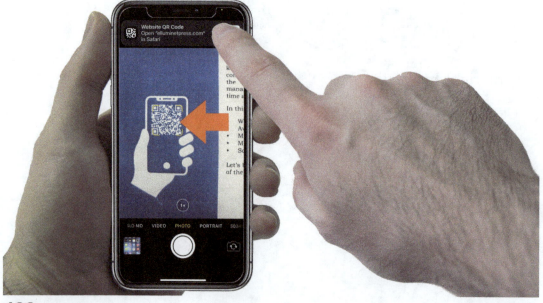

Android

To scan the code with your phone or tablet, open the camera app.

Frame the code in the middle of the screen. Tap on the website popup at the top.

If it doesn't scan, turn on 'Scan QR codes'. To do this, tap the settings icon on the top left. Turn on 'scan QR codes'.

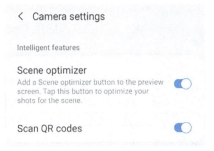

If the setting isn't there, you'll need to download a QR Code scanner. Open the Google Play Store, then search for "QR Code Scanner".

Index

SOMETHING
NOT COVERED?

We want to create the best possible resources to help you learn and get things done, so if we've missed anything out, then please get in touch using the links below and let us know. Thanks.

 office@elluminetpress.com

 elluminetpress.com/feedback

www.ingramcontent.com/pod-product-compliance
Lightning Source LLC
LaVergne TN
LVHW062316060326
832902LV00013B/2257